604c Huddersfield Road, Ravensthorpe
Dewsbury WF13 3HL
01924 500647
www.ihtlearning.co.uk
Vat Number 981 981 175   Com Reg 07512521

The i-learning revolution:

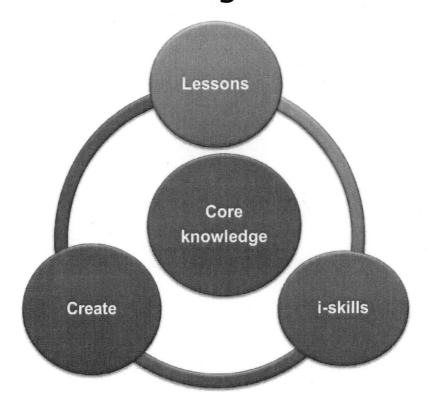

A new pedagogy

Bradley Lightbody

In-House Training
604c Huddersfield Road, Ravensthorpe
Dewsbury WF13 3HL
01924 500647
www.ihtlearning.co.uk
Vat Number 981 981 175   Com Reg 07512521

www.collegenet.co.uk

Publications

The **i**-learning revolution:
A new pedagogy

by

Bradley Lightbody M.Ed

A Collegenet publication, www.collegenet.co.uk
First published January 2012

First published January 2012 by:
Collegenet Limited
53 Windmill Lane
Batley
West Yorkshire
WF17 0NT
United Kingdom

A catalogue entry for this book is available from the British Library.
ISBN 978-0-9563245-1-1

Printed and bound in the United Kingdom
by CPI Antony Rowe, Chippenham, Wiltshire.
www.antonyrowe.co.uk

iv

The i-learning revolution: A new pedagogy

Acknowledgements	vii
Preface	ix
1. The knowledge Age	1
2. The internet revolution	16
3. The i-generations	36
4. Re-thinking the curriculum	56
5. 21st Century skills	80
6. A new pedagogy	100
7. Flipped learning	111
8. The learning portal	121
9. The independent learner	133
10. The i-Learning revolution	153
Appendix A	156
References	159

Acknowledgements

The author and publisher gratefully acknowledge the following for permission to reproduce copyright material.

Firstly, my gratitude to the Director of ncn High Pavement Sixth Form College, Martin Slattery for his commitment to innovation and to ILT Development Champion Andrew Edis for his many suggestions for improvement and his endless enthusiasm and energy. Also thanks to Syed Wajeeh of Fizaconsulting.co.uk for his patience, support and development of the software for the Learning Portal. Quacquarelli Symonds Ltd for permission to quote top university data. The Organisation for Economic co-operation and Development (OECD) for their permission to quote from a range of highly informative international research on different aspects of teaching and learning but in particular, Pisa reports and ILT developments. The Confederation of British Industry (CBI) for permission to quote employability skills surveys 2010 and 2011. Thanks are also due to the following organisations for their permission to reproduce their curriculum models, International Baccalaureate Organisation (IBO), Partnership for 21st Century Skills rainbow model, Cambridge International Examinations Pre-U model and Steve Bolingbroke of the Kunskapsskolan Education Programme (KED) consortium. Many thanks also to Chiki Okodo, Head of Education, World Skills London for an invitation to present a seminar at the World Skills championships in London October 2011 and for permission to reproduce the self employment Skills Wheel. Finally, I and all teachers, owe a considerable debt to Professor John Hattie of Auckland University for his detailed analysis of international research into effective teaching and learning as documented in his textbook Visible Learning 2009.

Every attempt has been made to contact all copyright holders and to gain responses but any omissions will be corrected and addressed on notification.

My deep thanks to my personal Generation Y members
Emma, Stuart, Gemma and Paul who keep me up-to-date and
to Carol for all her love and support
despite too many hours spent in front of a wordprocessor.

Preface

Our world is changing rapidly as the electronic age gathers momentum and alters and transforms everything it touches. The internet connected TV is a reality and soon the internet will take centre stage in our living rooms and offer the whole family a highly accessible window on the world. The internet offers unlimited choices of services, entertainment and information. However, it is the mobile connection to the internet via Smartphone and Tablet that will be truly transformational by placing a wealth of information and services literally at our fingertips. In the video rental shops nationwide they are waiting for the video market to move online as we increasingly upgrade to internet connected TVs and simply download films direct to the TV. In the bookshops they are similarly watching the movement of books online as the Kindle, Kobo and Ipad go mainstream and become the primary way to access and read books. Amazon already sells more ebooks than printed books. Many in education have yet to realise that their market is also ripe for download. Why wait for a lesson on Bismarck's foreign policy? A Google search will provide all you need to know in a matter of seconds with the significant majority of the hits from authoritative academic sources. However, how far was Bismarck's foreign policy a success or a failure? The answer to that question is the real learning, not the basic facts of Bismarck's career or policies, and coaching the answer is the real craft of teaching. What are the questions you wish your students to be able to answer? Specify them topic by topic, let the internet provide the facts and the lessons the analysis and the evaluation. The internet will liberate teachers from imparting basic factual information and our students from the chore of writing it down. Visit the Khan Academy www.khanacademy.org and glimpse a future that is already the present. Our pedagogy needs to rapidly shift to embrace independent or i-Learning because we are already falling behind the curve.

Bradley Lightbody
5th January 2012

1 The knowledge age

"the illiterate of the 21ˢᵗ Century will not be those who cannot read and write but those who cannot learn, unlearn and relearn".[1]

Alvin Toffler circa 1980

In 1970 the futurist thinker and sociologist, Alvin Toffler, published *Future Shock* which charted the rise of mass communication, mass culture and the emergence of a global economy as the consumer era gained pace. In the late 1970s the emergence of the silicon chip, with its fast and cheap processing power, raised the potential for modern personal computers to categorise, sort, search and process large volumes of information. Toffler made the far-sighted realisation that industrial society was on the cusp of fundamental change and in his book, *The Third Wave*, published in 1980, he postulated a movement away from industrial society into a 'super industrial age' or what other writers and thinkers referred to as the 'post-industrial society', the 'global society', the 'information society' or the 'electronic age'. Today the term the 'Knowledge Age' has gained currency to reflect the internet as 'oracle' and the rapid shift from 1.0 to 2.0 and now the fast emerging 3.0 level internet technology. However, although internet technology is new the term 'Knowledge Age' is not. In 1968 Professor Peter F Drucker (1909-2005) first published a seminal account of the changing patterns of work and society as the service sector advanced entitled, *The Age of Discontinuity.* Drucker knew nothing of computers but he devoted a whole section of his book to the rise of the Knowledge Age and lamented the failure of schools to move away from the formal classroom with its single speed '*I speak and you listen*' pedagogy. He observed that despite many centuries of technological and social change schools were largely unchanged and that the pedagogy of a modern school would be entirely familiar to a time-traveller from Mesopotamia circa 5000BC. Schools have traditionally made their focus obedience, regimentation and discipline rather than a love of learning, creativity and promoting how to learn. In the days of Socrates (470-399 B.C.), in Ancient Greece children sat in straight rows in strict silence to learn by rote with a slave the Paidagogeo (hence the term pedagogy) seated at the back of the classroom whose sole job was to lash anyone who displayed the slightest lapse in concentration. Corporal punishment was abolished in British schools in 1987 but it still remains legal in most parts of the world including many individual American States. Thousands of years later, since the time of Socrates, how far have we come? The traditional pedagogy of a teacher standing at the front of a classroom imparting basic information at fixed times, in a fixed order, to a fixed pace and in a fixed way is largely set in granite. However, the Web 2.0 and the emerging Web 3.0 are releasing unstoppable waves of online learning materials accessible 24-7. By 2020, at the latest, the profusion of authoritative online information will end the ancient role of the teacher as the gatekeeper of knowledge and usher in the i-learning revolution i.e. independent learners and realise Drucker's vision of autonomous guided learning. Granite teachers may remain but they will soon face empty classrooms if their lessons only provide basic, factual information. The accessibility of information online should be welcomed because it will free teachers to return to Socrates and to guide and facilitate learning i.e. questioning what students currently know and understand, examining their evidence, challenging them to justify and explain, identifying their misunderstandings and finally coaching all in small groups and one to one to achieve their full potential. The future of teaching is less gatekeeper and more gateway.

The Third Wave

Toffler advanced that in the Western world the industrial age that had commenced with the Industrial Revolution in England (circa 1750) was at an end and that the world's advanced industrial economies were embarking upon a third major wave of economic development.

- First wave – agrarian
- Second wave - industrial
- Third wave - post industrial

Toffler's first wave identified the switch from a Hunter-Gatherer based society to an agrarian society when early man realised that instead of spending long hours hunting game it was preferable to trap and breed captive animals and thereby create a controlled and reliable source of food. Likewise rather than regularly scour large tracts of forest for edible fruits, nuts, berries and roots it was preferable to clear the forest and to propagate whole fields of the relevant plants and trees to create a readily accessible and more abundant food supply. Today a few hunter-gather based nomadic societies still survive unchanged in parts of Borneo, Africa and the Amazon Basin. Toffler's second wave, the industrial revolution, commenced circa 1750 in England when a series of inventions within the weaving trade, notably Hargreaves Spinning Jenny, significantly increased the productive capacity of a single weaver. The assembly of hundreds of machines and weavers within a single building (factory) gave rise to the mechanised factory system and prompted the large scale movement of people off the land into towns and ultimately cities. This movement was underpinned by the application of steam power which revolutionised transport and mechanised agriculture and replaced human labour in the fields with more productive and tireless machines. Today the majority of the world's nations are industrial. Out of the 192 nations recognised by the United Nations only six have economies with more than 50% of their economic activity arising from agriculture and all are in Africa. The country with highest percentage of its economic activity within the agrarian sector is Liberia with 76.9% of its national income largely linked to rubber and timber harvesting[2]. Toffler's third wave predicted the widespread application of computer technology, automation and new forms of energy generation and communication. Toffler was aware of and experimented with the first microcomputers on the market like the best selling Commodore PET microcomputer (1977-82) which offered the public games and businesses wordprocessing and data management. However, Toffler was certainly a futurist because whereas he knew nothing of the mobile or cell phone (first appearance Japan 1979 followed by USA 1983) or the Internet (1991) he recognised the potential of cheap, computer technology to transform business and society. Today the electronic society he predicted is a firm reality and computers are an everyday indispensable tool for work, leisure and increasingly learning.

The global economy

Toffler's vision has been underwritten by the rise of a global economy and a more interconnected and interdependent world. We are less conscious of national boundaries and connected by global brands, international sporting competitions (the past two managers of the English Football Team were not English), international charitable and welfare organisations, the International Court of Justice, European Union, World Bank, World Trade Organisation, 24 hour global news coverage, international cuisine, the United Nations, the Olympic Games, the G8 and G20 economic summits and within education the World Skills Championships which recognise and celebrate our students' highest skill achievements www.worldskills.org. In addition, the increasing medium of English Language and common global concerns e.g. sustainability, the environment and human rights and the all-pervasive internet have all contributed to a global 24/7 connected community. Twitter alone has given a voice to many ordinary people and transcended national boundaries and connected people worldwide. A simple video uploaded to You Tube can command a world-wide audience and be transformative. Google is now a recognised global brand second only to Coca Cola in public recognition tests.

Top ten economies

The 192 nations recognised by the United Nations are all at different stages of economic, political and social development. The top ten world economies by the standard economic measure of Gross Domestic Product (total value of all goods and services) are as listed below.

Figure 1. Top ten world economies by GDP 2010[3]

No	Country	GDP trillions	Agriculture %	Industry %	Service %
1	United States	14.66	1.1	22.1	76.8
2	China	10.09	10.2	46.9	43.0
3	Japan	4.31	1.4	24.9	73.8
4	India	4.06	18.5	26.3	55.2
5	Germany	2.94	0.9	27.8	71.3
6	Russia	2.22	4.0	36.8	59.1
7	United Kingdom	2.173	0.7	21.8	77.5
8	Brazil	2.172	5.8	26.8	67.4
9	France	2.145	2.0	18.5	79.5
10	Italy	1.774	1.9	25.3	72.8
Average			4.6	27.7	67.6

Source CIA Factbook 2011

The wealthiest nation in the world, by far, is the United States but if income is adjusted against debt many would argue that China is on track to overtake the United States as the world's highest performing economy and as the economy with the greatest potential for future growth. Both the Beijing Olympics 2008 and the Shanghai World Expo 2010 showcased to the world Chinese expertise and ambition. The latter was a potent symbol of change. The very first world expo was the Great Exhibition held in London 1851 when Great Britain displayed and confirmed her dominance as the world's greatest economic and military power. China hosted its first world expo in 1999 appropriately entitled, *'Marching into the 21st Century'* whereas in Shanghai 2010 the U.S. pavilion understandably countered with the slogan, *'Rising to the Challenge'*. The rise of China has been monumental. In 1990 China did not have a single motorway but today China has the world's second biggest motorway network at 47,000 miles and the skyscrapers of Beijing and Shanghai rival New York. The future challenge is perhaps high technology as evidenced by the dominance of robots and robotic applications at Expo 2010. It was perhaps no coincidence that shortly after Expo 2010 commenced a robotic first was claimed when a robot manufactured by Kokoro in Japan conducted the wedding ceremony for Satoko Inoue and Tomohiro Shibata (employees of Kokoro). However, the Kokoro robot can only interact against a narrow pre-programmed script and we still await the full breakthrough into artificial intelligence. In 1941 as the U.S. economy boomed Time magazine declared the Twentieth Century to be the 'American Century' but by 2030 it is highly likely that we will start to speak of the 'Chinese Century'. However, India is also on course to be a global economic power with high future growth prospects given the size of its young and increasingly well-qualified (and English speaking) workforce. The most significant economic trend, across the western world, is the sharp rise in Service Sector employment. The average size of the Service Sector across the major world economies is 67.6% but it is much higher among the advanced economies of the western world as indicated in Figure 1. A significant employment switch has occurred within the last thirty years following the commitment of most western economies, including the USA, to Free Trade and the removal of high import duties on foreign goods. The common goal was to reduce living costs by permitting cheaper goods to reach the high street rather than maintaining artificially high prices. The West immediately gained a

- Nothing is more American than blue jeans but in 2004 the last Levi Strauss plant in the USA closed and all production moved East – at its height Levi Strauss employed 37,000 workers.

There are many hundreds of examples of such job losses across manufacturing industry and it is estimated that over the last ten years a minimum of 7 million manufacturing jobs have been lost in the United States to overseas competition, 4.5 million in the UK and many more millions across Europe. As industries closed or relocated significant pockets of high unemployment arose and blighted many towns where once a coal mine, steel mill, car factory etc provided steady and reliable work for each generation. In addition those industries provided many unskilled or low skilled employment opportunities for those who left High School with few or no qualifications. Today a 'lost' generation of young people with few qualifications and no job opportunities stand on many of our street corners at high personal and social cost. In England they are designated Neets (Not in Employment, Education or Training) and their numbers in 2011 are currently at a significant high of 1.163 million. They lack the skills and qualifications to enter the high skilled service and technology sectors which dominate the employment market. This is a significant challenge for schools and colleges to equip young people with the knowledge and crucially the skills required to be successful within the 21st Century job market.

The high skilled service sector

In the Western world today the jobs are in the dominant Service Sector. In the UK the National Strategy Skills audit 2010 identified the following top ten areas of employment and economic growth:[4]

1. Business services
2. Health and social care
3. Retail
4. Hotels and catering
5. Miscellaneous services
6. Construction
7. Computing and related services
8. Education
9. Banking and finance
10. Transport and storage

In first position for predicted growth is Business Services which includes Accountancy, Law, Insurance, Advertising, Public Relations, Recruitment, Cleaning, Technical Support, Information Services, IT Support etc. Business services has grown by 238% since 1991 and in 2010 accounted for 20% of Britain's GDP, employing some 3.2 million people equivalent to 11% of all employment. In contrast the Manufacturing sector which dominated employment in the 1960s and 70s has shrunk to 11% of GDP. Beyond the top ten there are significant employment opportunities in Tourism, Media, Arts, Sports, Leisure, Personal Services and Fashion. Service Sector jobs demand a more highly skilled workforce and place pressure on schools and universities to ensure that young people possess not only good basic skills but also high information technology, interpersonal and intrapersonal skills. The significance of the Service Sector in terms of current and future employment may be gauged by the share of Service Sector employment across the Organisation for Economic Co-operation and Development (OECD) member states. The OECD was founded in 1961 to co-ordinate and promote economic growth across the world's leading democratic and free market economies. From an original 20 member states in 1961 the OECD has expanded to 31 members with Chile the latest signatory on 7th May 2010. The member states are listed below in rank order of Service Sector employment from highest to lowest.

Figure 2. OECD member states service sector size [5]

No	Country	Service %	Industry %	Agriculture %
1	Luxembourg	86.0	13.6	0.4
2	France	79.5	18.5	2.0
3	Greece	78.8	17.9	3.3
4	United Kingdom	77.5	21.8	0.7
5	Belgium	77.4	21.9	0.7
6	United States	76.8	22.1	1.1
7	Denmark	76.6	22.1	1.2
8	Portugal	74.7	22.9	2.4
9	Japan	73.8	24.9	1.4
10	Italy	72.8	25.3	1.9
11	Netherlands	72.5	24.9	2.6
12	Sweden	71.6	26.6	1.9

No	Country	Service %	Industry %	Agriculture %
13	Canada	71.5	26.3	2.2
14	Germany	71.3	27.8	0.9
15	Switzerland	71.1	27.7	1.3
16	New Zealand	71.0	24.3	4.7
17	Spain	70.7	26.0	3.3
18	Australia	70.5	25.6	3.9
19	Ireland	70.0	29.0	2.0
20	Iceland	69.9	24.6	5.5
21	Austria	69.4	29.2	1.5
22	Finland	68.1	29.0	2.9
23	Turkey	63.8	26.6	9.6
24	Mexico	63.5	32.6	3.9
25	Poland	63.4	33.0	3.5
26	Hungary	60.5	37	2.4
27	Czech Republic	60	37.6	2.4
28	South Korea	58.2	39.3	2.6
29	Norway	58.1	39.4	2.5
30	Chile	53.1	41.8	5.1
Average		70.7	27.3	2.6

CIA Factbook 2011 Note: no data available for Slovakia hence 30 countries listed rather than 31.

The OECD average for Service Sector employment is 70.7% slightly lower than the European Union average of 73.1%. The UK is in 4th position with 77.5% of economic activity Service Sector based. A prominent example of the rising Service Sector in the UK is fashion which accounts for 2.7% of UK GDP at £21 billion and when related retail is added in £37 billion. This is three times the worth of UK car manufacture or the chemical industry and has created jobs for 1.3 million people. Beyond the OECD member states Hong Kong emerges as the world's highest Service Sector based economy at 92.5% of all employment (note – whereas Hong Kong is an autonomous economic region it is a province of China rather than a separate state). The breakdown for the other significant economic powers who are non members of the OECD is as follows:

Figure 3 sample of Non OECD economies service sectors[6]

Country	Service %	Industry %	Agriculture %
Brazil	67.4	26.8	5.8
India	55.2	26.3	18.5
Russia	59.1	36.8	4.0
China	43.0	46.9	10.2
South Africa	66.7	30.8	2.5

The clear trend across the developed world is for most jobs to be within the highly skilled Service Sector. Within the Service Sector IT is a significant employer across the OECD economies at an average of 21%. The employment percentages range from a high of 30.6% for Luxembourg down to a low of 11.8% for Turkey. The United Kingdom is second in the rank order at 28% and United States is relatively far down the rank order in 21st position with 20.2% of its Service Sector employment directly related to IT.

Population size

A qualifying factor to consider is population size because growth in the Service Sector is dependent upon a flow of highly skilled graduates, in particular, and therefore the number of graduates within the labour force becomes significant. Here both China and India enjoy a major advantage because with ever expanding education systems they are creating a deep reservoir of able young people. The top ten countries by size of population are as listed:

Figure 4 Top ten countries by size of population July 2009[7]

No.	Country	Population
1	China	1,336,718,015
2	India	1,89,172,906
3	United States	313,232,044
4	Indonesia	245,613,043
5	Brazil	203,429,773
6	Pakistan	187,342,721
7	Bangladesh	158,570,535
8	Nigeria	155,215,573
9	Russia	138,739,892
10	Japan	126,475,664

Source CIA Factbook 2011

10

If a genius is one in a million then China has 1,336, India 1,89, United States 313 and so on. In comparison the United Kingdom has a low population of 62,698,362 but the European Union has a population of 492,387,344 and this confirms its significance as a major economic marketplace. However, a significant advantage shared by the United Kingdom, Europe and the United States is a well-developed Higher Education sector. The rank order of the world's leading universities, across a range of standard criteria, is as listed below in Figure 5.

Figure 5 Top ten leading world universities 2011[8]

No.	University	Country
1	University of Cambridge	UK
2	Harvard University	USA
3	Massachusetts Institute of Technology	USA
4	Yale	USA
5	University of Oxford	UK
6	Imperial College London	UK
7	UCL (University College of London)	UK
8	University of Chicago	USA
9	University of Pennsylvania	USA
10	Columbia University	USA

Source: QS Quacquarelli Symonds (www.topuniversities.com).

The United States holds six of the top ten positions and the United Kingdom four. The first university from outside the USA or UK to appear in the list is McGill University, Canada in 17th place closely followed by ETH Zurich in Switzerland in 18th place. The first Asian university on the list is Hong Kong in 22nd place and after that Tokyo in 25th place. The high quality of American and British universities is based upon a development time measured in hundreds of years whereas the Chinese and Indian Higher Education sectors are still relatively young. Quality and performance in terms of research and research that translates into patents and patents into new technology takes time and money. On 6th May 2010 the Chinese Premier, Wen Jiabo presented a ten year development plan 2010-2020, *'National programme for long term reform and development'* to focus on the expansion of high quality education across China supported by a rise in education spending to 4% of GDP. This is a low percentage in comparison to the West but once again numbers matter and 4% of the Chinese GDP is a big number. Jiabo also set a target for 310 million scientists and engineers to be engaged in

R&D by 2020 compared to the existing base of 161 million. China currently has 2,263 universities and the university entrance tests include fluency in English for admittance. As a result of this policy an estimated 300 million Chinese now speak English making China paradoxically the largest English speaking country in the world. Where do they learn English? Largely from *avatars* on websites like *www.speak2me.cn* which permit young people anywhere to learn at their own pace and in their own time. This delivers basic fluency before many choose to specialise and enrol in formal English language lessons. The spread of this type of website highlights how Web technology is being embedded in China. The current estimate of internet users across China is 384 million, 180 million maintain a blog and at least 700 million possess a mobile/cell phone. China has successfully industrialised and by 2020 it has set significant goals for entry into the Service Sector and the Knowledge Age. The challenge for China is to maintain social and political stability as more and more well-educated young people who know nothing of the Long March but are well aware of events in Tiananmen Square question the primacy of the Communist Party and seek a democratic revolution. Google withdrew its services from China in 2010 following its refusal to comply with strict government censorship of web searches. India is also advancing rapidly and both India and China have young populations who are more likely to be computer literate and ready to take advantage of Knowledge Age employment compared to the largely ageing populations in the Western world. Japan, in particular, has an aging population with 36% of the population predicted to be over 75 by the year 2015. As both China and India prosper Service Sector jobs can and may follow manufacturing jobs East as the new Knowledge Age economy takes hold. Ashmount Primary School in London already employs Indian graduates to deliver online one to one maths tuition for any of its pupils who need extra support. The pupils communicate with their tutor 4,000 miles away by headset and answer questions on their computer screens. It is fairly common for primary children to link to children in other parts of the world via the internet when completing projects and so the extension into online tuition is perhaps not such a major step.

The knowledge Age

The Service Sector is sustained by fast, reliable information processing, retrieval and communication but this can all be delivered over the internet and by video conferencing technology as required. A significant number of Smartphones include an option for video calls with Apple the market leader. Distance is not an issue for the internet or a video enabled smartphone and websites like gotomeeting.com provide an instant video conference facility for business. Perhaps many of us work for companies or schools, colleges or universities with an accounting department but how often do you need to physically enter the Accounts Office for a face to face discussion? Perhaps you are actively discouraged from doing so for reasons of security. Consequently it is common for budget or payroll queries to be answered by telephone, email or via secure password controlled information on the company intranet without any direct contact with the accounts staff. So could the accounts be outsourced to a remote accountancy firm? This is already a reality for many firms and perhaps also within our private lives. In 2010 58% of internet users were registered for online banking. A telephone enquiry in relation to our telephone, broadband, credit card, insurance or bank account etc may be answered by an operative in Mumbai. Most of India's young IT graduates also speak English but earn a sixth of the wage of a Western IT graduate and so jobs that only a few years ago would have been in New York, Boston, London or Manchester have already shifted East. On 2nd June 2011 Birmingham City Council announced the transfer of its IT support division to Mumbai with the loss of 120 jobs. The value of the Call Centre industry to India in 2009 was $12.5 billion. Some of the Call Centre jobs are relatively low skilled but there are also many high skilled 'knowledge' jobs across Banking, Finance, Management, Sales, Law, Computing etc. Knowledge of this type is highly portable and is easily transferred to a customer across the internet. Many ordinary people have stumbled into global commerce by the simple act of buying or selling on Ebay or Amazon. The customer or supplier might be anywhere in the world but with the internet and a reliable postage system it does not matter if the customer is in the next town or a different country. Scale that up to company level and we can have virtual companies that only exist on the internet but will supply goods or services at the touch of a button. Within the UK there are now 159 'virtual' companies with an annual turnover above one million pounds and all started by ordinary people. E-retail *clicks not bricks* is fast expanding with a 14% growth in online purchases 2010 while offline shops are seeing falling sales because their overheads mean higher prices at the till. Amazon is the best known E-retailer. However, perhaps you buy your groceries online from *Ocado.com* or use the Ocado App from Apple which offers the entire stock of 21,000 grocery choices for purchase over your smartphone? Or perhaps you are one of the 7 million people who shop for clothes at *Asos.com* each month? Asos is a virtual business founded in 2000 and it has expanded rapidly with revenues up by 35% to £223 million and customers by 25%. Asos specialises in fashion for the age-group 14-35 and in the case of dresses alone stocks 4,000 styles compared to the 150 available in a typical high street shop. Or go to *made.com* to buy furniture at 50-80% less than the high street. Many ordinary people have also discovered Skype and the joy and quality of 'no cost' video or audio calls to friends and relatives around the world. At peak times 23 million callers are chatting on Skype. Businesses can connect just as easily and with superior equipment and software. Knowledge workers only need a laptop and/or a smartphone and increasingly just the smartphone. By 2012 sales of smartphones are expected to overtake laptops as business users discover the highly portable smartphone can satisfy all of their communication and information processing needs. Why spend two hours to commute into London from your home to sit at a desk to answer the telephone, to answer your emails and/or to write and send a report when all that can be done just as easily from your home or Starbucks or Waterstones or sitting in a park? Many businesses with highly expensive offices in city centres are down-sizing and encouraging their staff to work from home and/or 'hot desk'. By 2013 it is estimated by the research company IDC that 75.5% of USA professionals will be mobile, 74.5% in Japan and 50.3% in Western Europe. Instead of waiting to retire to the countryside for a slower pace of life why not move now but carry on working? The company *Regus.co.uk* offers, for hire by the day, week or month, fully furnished office spaces, IT facilities and virtual office staff i.e. receptionists to answer your telephone, forward post etc in 450 cities in 75 countries. Therefore virtual companies can come down to earth whenever they need to. Why wait for someone to give you a recording contract? In 2004 an aspiring musician, Lily Allen, posted demos of her music on Myspace and in 2006 her debut single *Smile* went to the top of the British charts and worldwide success. Similarly the mother of 14 year old Justin Bieber from Ontario, Canada posted a video of him on *You Tube* singing the song '*One time*' for wider family to access and view. The video went viral and was viewed 10 million times in seven months and Justin has since become a global star with two million sales of his debut album, *'My world'*. The Knowledge Age can empower the individual just as much as the large corporation and provide an outlet for individual creativity. In 2006 the then Senator Barack Obama highlighted the challenge raised by the Knowledge Age in a speech in Chicago entitled, '21st century schools for a 21st century economy' , *"We now live in a world where the most valuable skill you can sell is knowledge. Revolutions in technology and communication have created an entire economy of high-tech, high-wage jobs that can be located anywhere there's an internet connection. And today, a child in Chicago is not only competing for jobs with one in Boston, but thousands more in Bangalore and Beijing who are being educated longer and better than ever before"* [9]. The inference is the importance of building skills as well as knowledge and it is important for schools and colleges to build the skills required by the dominant Service and hi-tech sectors and to track back to the classroom in terms of how we prepare young people to compete within a global marketplace. This should include guidance on self-employment and prompts to creativity because self-employment can lead to employment for others and we must not overlook that many of our leading entrepreneurs like James Dyson started out with a single creative idea. Our future prosperity will be built or lost by the rising i-generations Y and Z and they will need an education system that fosters high interpersonal and intrapersonal skills as well as knowledge if they are to succeed in the Knowledge Age.

2 The internet explosion

You perhaps never noticed it but 8th June 2011 was Internet Protocol Version 6 (IPv6) day or more popularly the internet 'big bang'. IPv6 represented a significant landmark and explosion in the scale and reach of the internet. The launch of IPv6 created a deep reservoir of 340 trillion, trillion, trillion unique internet addresses. That is a big number. In the 1980s the internet was launched with four billion unique addresses and at the time four billion seemed like an impossibly large number but by 2010 only 14% of those addresses remained unassigned. No one had anticipated devices beyond

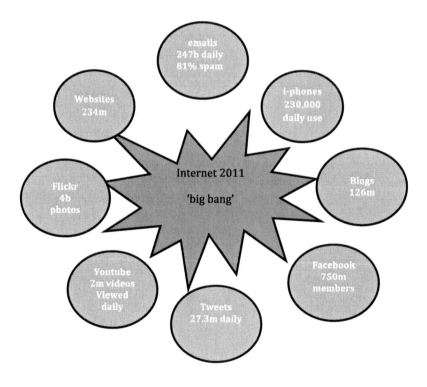

computers needing to be connected to the internet but with the development of internet linked mobiles/cell phones, game consoles, e-readers, Sat Navs, home security cameras and digital televisions etc the internet was facing a physical limit to its growth. Any device connected to the internet must have a unique IP address for identification so that data can be correctly routed. The progressive shift to IPv6 will hopefully resolve the problem and create a robust infrastructure for our rapidly expanding electronic world, aided by a significant increase in the number of internet servers and the roll-out of 4G superfast mobile broadband.

Internet evolution

The internet we all know (as opposed to early secure U.S. military communication channels) was developed by the British scientist Tim Berners-Lee in 1989 to solve the problem of large data transfers between scientists working on the Cern project (particle physics research) in Geneva, Switzerland. The internet with its http (hyper text transfer protocol) prefix went live to the public on 6th August

Web 1.0 1995-2004 Information Web	Web 2.0 2005-8 Interactive web	Web 3.0 2009+ Semantic Web
• Dial-up	• Broadband	• Wireless Wi-Fi
• Read-only	• Interactive	• Create / add
• Tower computer	• Laptop	• Tablet e.g. ipad
• Floppy discs	• MP3 players / ipod	• Smart phone
• Powerpoint	• PS2 / Xbox	• Netbooks
• Instant messaging	• Ebay	• Blogs
• Word	• Amazon	• E-book readers
• Excel	• Online shopping	• Cloud computing
• Powerpoint	• Online travel	• Robots
• Clipart	• Google	• Smart homes
• Email	• Digital camera	• Smart cars
• Email attachments	• Podcasts	• GPS position
• BBC	• iplayer	• Avatars
• AOL	• Wikipedia	• 3D
• Yahoo	• Twitter	• TV-i convergence
• Company websites	• Facebook	• Motion sensors
• Museum collections	• You Tube	• 4G high speed
• Art galleries	• Flickr	• Near field apps
• Charity websites	• Sat Nav	• The Grid
• Government	• Online banking	• Apps
• Cash machines	• RSS	• Augmented reality

1991. Perhaps this date will become the 1066 or 1766 of future generations? In only twenty years the internet has revolutionised all aspects of life and work across the western world. The rapid development of the internet is marked in terms of 1.0, 2.0 and 3.0 evolutionary stages. The examples listed above are not all internet developments but include examples of applications and key websites to provide context.

The 1.0 stage was the early internet and personal computer age circa 1995 when our relationship was largely one of access and passively receiving information in the same way we accessed traditional television, radio, newspapers, books etc. Websites added to this list in a largely 'read only' relationship. Although there was some interaction as Microsoft Messenger and other instant messaging (IM) services became very popular. In terms of wider technology most people in employment mastered the popular Microsoft Office suite of programs (*programs* is the correct spelling for software and *programmes* for all other meanings) or equivalent for wordprocessing, presentations, data management, design etc and discovered the ease and speed of email. A rush of information orientated websites provided a revolution in the ease of access to museum collections, art galleries and Government departments etc. This was followed by companies establishing internet websites but largely for contact and information provision rather than online selling. This was largely because the 1.0 internet was too slow due to its reliance upon dial-up technology. The low rate of data transfer largely precluded downloads of video, photographs and graphics because they were too byte heavy. Perhaps you can still remember that distinctive sound of the internet connecting over your telephone line and once connected watching and waiting as the text and graphics slowly unfurled. Web site designers often advised business clients to avoid graphics because they would take too long to download or, for speed, they integrated a clickable text only version of the website. Perhaps the one key transformation that early computer technology gave us was debit cards and the *'hole-in-the-wall'* cash machine invented by John Shepherd-Barron (1925-2010) in 1967 although it took until the early 1980s before they became widespread. Debit cards are now so integrated into our lives that it is difficult to remember when we last queued to a bank counter with a cheque made out to 'cash' or wrote a cheque in the supermarket to pay for our weekly shopping. Web

1.0 was expensive with payment by the minute and this meant no one browsed for too long and magazines were full of tips of how to download and read off line. Surfing the internet, in most households, was often a stressful experience because parents stood over their children with a stopwatch but with the arrival of Web 2.0 all of that stress melted away.

Web 2.0 the interactive web

The Web 2.0 technology arrived circa 2005 with broadband – the permanently switched on internet that ended dial-up. Broadband connected a fat digital highway to our computers rather than the narrow country lane of Web 1.0 and permitted a much richer content to be downloaded. The connections were also stable. It was frustratingly common in the 1.0 era to lose the connection before a file had finished its download. Web 2.0 opened-up all manner of interactive applications with the major categories:

- Online shopping
- Online banking
- Travel
- Maps
- Information
- Media
- Music
- Gaming
- Social networks

Today the majority of businesses maintain a website. It would be regarded as unusual not to do so and this in itself is a mark of the internet revolution. However, whereas in the Web 1.0 world the content was largely company information and contact details the Web 2.0 world has introduced interactive live transactions as standard. Buying goods and services online with a credit card has become a norm and many people have also opened online banking accounts attracted by the ease of access and 24/7 money management. We can also make bookings and purchase tickets online for just about anything. Can you remember the days when you walked into a railway station and queued to buy a train ticket before *thetrainline.com* came along? Where would we all be without *Amazon.com* which delivers any book (and now many more products) often within 24 hours of order? Amazon is a $24 billion retailer and so perhaps it is unsurprising that the Borders bookshop chain closed in December 2009. In June 2010 the Oxford University Press announced that the Oxford English Dictionary, which has been the definitive guide to the English Language since its first publication in 1879, will no longer be printed on paper and the next edition will be an entirely digital publication. The travel industry was revolutionised by the ability to self-book hotels and flights via websites like *Lastminute.com* and *Expedia.com* rather than queuing to speak to a travel agent and today 34% of the world travel business has moved online with the UK the market leader. Websites like *tripadvisor.com* and *Wikitravel.org* report our recommendations and grumbles and permit a glimpse behind the glossy brochures. In 2009 Google commissioned research by the Boston Consulting Group to chart the level of online buying and selling in the UK. The data showed that 62% of UK adults bought goods or services online in 2009. Buying online is now a £50 billion a year industry in the UK making it a bigger contributor to the UK economy than Education, Health, Transport or Construction. If the internet was listed as a sector of the UK economy then would be in fifth place by Gross Domestic Product (GDP):

Real Estate and Business services (23%),

Manufacturing (12%),

Wholesale and Retail (11%),

Financial services (9%)

Online sales (7.2%).

The value of online sales is predicted to reach 10% of GDP by 2015. However, among the developed world economies the UK is in sixth position for the overall value of trading and shopping online. The top fifteen countries for online spending in 2009 were:[2]

NO.	Country	e-intensity index100 = average
1	Denmark	140
2	Republic of Korea	139
3	Japan	138
4	Sweden	134
5	Netherlands	129
6	United Kingdom	128
7	Norway	125
8	Finland	124
9	Germany	120
10	Iceland	111
11	United States	109
12	Luxembourg	109
13	Australia	108
14	France	105
15	Austria	103

Source: Boston Consulting Group 2010

It is inevitable that advertising would follow any increase in online buying and in a significant confirmation of the importance of the internet the amount spent on online advertising overtook the amount spent on TV advertising in the first quarter of 2011. The atlas has come alive with Google Earth permitting us to zoom down from space to any spot on the Earth's surface and now with Streetview the ability to 'walk' through a video capture of a city or perhaps your street. Try entering your postcode and see if you've been mapped yet? The Sat Nav has replaced map reading in our cars and transport industry and also on foot via our mobile or cell phones for city centre street navigation or even hiking up a mountainside. In terms of finding information few of us now visit a library or open a set of encyclopaedias because of the ease of using Google or one of the other major search engines like Ask, Jeeves, Altavista, Metacrawler, Gopher, Bing, About and Lycos. In addition, Wolframalpha.com is not a search engine but a vast storehouse of facts covering every major discipline and all verified by experts in their field. Even very basic information like finding a recipe for Rosti potatoes is faster online than trawling though your collection of recipe books. In seconds you will find a selection of recipes and often provided free by leading chefs. Google was founded in 1998 and is already a $120 billion corporation and in April 2010 it logged 4.1 billion search requests in the UK alone. Google images now holds 10 billion photographs so essentially if the person, place or object has been photographed then you will find it on Google. Searches for images are currently running at over one billion searches per day. Google has become a verb and it has transformed our lives and more than anything else ushered in the Knowledge Age. Anything you want to know is out there. In 2009, 47 million websites were added to the internet bringing the total number to an estimated 234 million websites. Apart from Google 68 million searches a month are made on *wikipedia.org*. Wikipedia now has 3,286,000 articles in English and over 10 million when other languages are included. Wikipedia articles all have been created by ordinary, interested people who have specialist knowledge they are willing to share. Some regard this as a weakness but Wikipedia has responded by ensuring that all articles are underpinned by verifiable references. The option is also there for those who spot a mistake to edit and correct it. So if you are a teacher or a subject expert take up the challenge and help to build a world-wide learning community. If you wish full academic confidence then *Britannica.com* remains the significant source with full comprehensive information on all major topics. Britannica also offers an App for mobile access on smartphones and tablets. Google Scholar is not as well-known but it provides a search portal to reliable academic information sources and *Learningportal.com* offers a gateway to university resources plus the range of quirky Ted videos and the celebrated *Khanacademy.org.* Web 2.0 has overturned fixed broadcast and print schedules with television, radio, newspapers and magazines accessible 24/7. The 24 hour news channels and world news summaries are now a staple and the BBC website, in particular, along with applications like the BBC iplayer offers a 'pull' rather than 'push' media relationship. The web has also revolutionised our relationship with music along with the development of the MP3 player and digital downloads. In 1999 the 18 year old American student Shawn Fanning created the music 'share' website Napster which permitted the electronic sharing of digital music tracks for download to an MP3 player. Napster was soon handling 3 billion downloads per month swiftly followed by a law suit from the disgruntled record industry that was watching with alarm as their sales plummeted. In 2001 Napster lost the law suit and was closed but it has since reopened as a legal commercial website by ending its download facility. Visit *napster.co.uk* and you can select tracks for streaming to your computer from what essentially is an online electronic jukebox. The website *spotify.com* offers a similar and rival service. In 2001 the market for music downloads was seized by Apple with the highly creative development of the ipod designed by the late Steve Jobs (1955-2011). In October 2010 Sony finally bowed to the dominance of digital music by ceasing production of the Walkman cassette player which was first launched in July 1979. Sony sold 220 million Walkmans over 30 years but it took Apple less than ten years to sell 250 million ipods. The intuitively, easy to operate, ipod has generated an even more lucrative income for Apple because of music purchases from the linked *itunes.com* music store. In the UK there have been over 500 million singles sold online since 2004 with a rapid year on year increase rising from 5.8 million in 2004 to 148.8 million in 2009. CD sales are falling sharply with just 3 million sold in the UK in 2009 and the most popular downloaded track? The answer is, '*I Gotta Feeling*' by the Black Eyed Peas. The music sector is worth £3.9 billion to the UK economy. Games are also big business. Ask your students or children their favourite game? Most adults, including most teachers, do not play computer games and tend to walk past the games shops on the high street and remain locked into the board games of their youth. However, you are walking past a multi-billion dollar business with gamers spending $22 billion on new games worldwide in 2009 including £1.79 billion in the UK alone. That was more than was spent on music or going to the cinema in the same time period. The most popular games platforms are Microsoft Xbox and Sony Playstation but in 2009 Wii stole the Christmas market with the launch of active 'on your feet' participation games, controlled by waving a wand. Wii Play has sold 27.4 million units, Wii Fit 21.6 million and Wii Sports a further 16 million units. However, to demonstrate that a year is a long time for technology Microsoft responded to the Wii challenge at Christmas 2010 with the development of the X-Box Kinect. The Kinect reads and tracks body movements without the need for a hand held wand and sparked a host of new gaming applications including 3D. How soon will it be before the Startrek 'hollowdeck' becomes a reality? *Farmville.com* is a virtual farm that players have to expand to make a profit by growing crops and raising livestock. It is played by 83 million people importance. Facebook also offers teachers and students a closed question and answer forum for supporting learning. Twitter was launched in 2006 and has fast become an internet phenomenon with 100 million registered 'tweeters'. In August 2010 the 20 billionth tweet was sent. Twitter is essentially an internet text message service with each message limited to 140 characters. The texts can be open to anyone to view otherwise restricted to you own list of recipients. The most widely followed tweeter in 2011 was Lady Gaga who has attracted 15,430,788 people to follow, read and respond to her tweets. In the UK the media personality Steven Fry also enjoys a large following. Twitter is largely everyday trivia but it has now reached the rate of 27.3 million tweets per day as people share what they are doing and thinking. If Twitter offers instant messaging then blogging is essentially an online diary and this too has become an internet phenomenon. The term blog is a corruption of weblog and in 2009 126 million bloggers were registered with the blogger search engine Technorati. Anyone can become a blogger and share their musings on any topic via websites like *blogger.com* or *wordpress.com*. Most are written by ordinary people like Weebirdy in Sydney who blogs on her daily life, some are by famous people like Sarah Brown who chartered the end of her husband's premiership in the UK or trend commentators like Pete Cashmore (mashable.com) who attracts seven million hits a month. The motivation is often as simple as saying 'I exist' but many companies and organisations publish blogs to chart developments, pop stars may blog to keep in contact with their fan base and writers, artists, scientists etc may blog to highlight their work and invite feedback from others in the same field etc. Blogs linked to your sphere of working might be beneficial because they will keep you in touch with the latest developments in a particular field of science, theatre, music, technology, catering etc as it happens. Most British politicians for instance will follow the political blogger Paul Staines or Guido Fawkes as he is better known because he has a reputation for hearing all of the Westminster gossip. Approximately 2 million people a month visit his blog at *order-order.com*. In the United States the *drudgereport.com* exercises a similar hold over American politics and/or the Huffington post. Why wait for a newspaper or a TV reporter to report what is happening when you can go direct to the source? RSS feeds or *Really Simple Syndication* denoted by a small orange square on participating websites are also highly popular. They offer what is essentially a news flash when something new of interest has been added to a website. This eases repetitive visits to websites by providing an immediate alert to something new. The RSS feeds can also be attached to particular sub topics of interest or to specialist blogs of interest and help to filter the mass of information available on the internet. Finally no commentary on Web 2.0 would be complete without mentioning You Tube which has been part of our lives since 2005. Anyone can send You Tube a video and they currently upload about 70,000 new video contributions a day and in terms of viewing one billion (yes one billion) people visit and view videos each day. At first You Tube had a reputation for hosting frivolous and unsavoury content but this has been significantly reduced and You Tube now includes lots of useful academic content. This has been strengthened by the release of *Youtube.com/teachers* as a dedicated library of teacher selected videos plus a personal online repository for your own selected videos. All of this makes for a vast Web 2.0. In 2011 the Web was estimated to hold 295 exabytes of data i.e. text, photographs, graphics and video. We are perhaps all familiar with the measure gigabyte but less so with the measure exabyte. The language of digital data measurement is as follows:

Rise of the Exabyte	
8 bits	1 byte
1024 bytes	1 kilobyte (KB)
1024 (KB)	1 megabyte (MB)
1024 (MB)	1 gigabyte (GB)
1024 (GB)	1 terabyte (TB)
1024 (TB)	1 petabyte (PB)
1024 (PB)	1 Exabyte (XB)

The storage and processing capacity of personal computers of the 1.0 era was measured in kilobytes but today gigabytes is the new standard. This explosion of data within Web 2.0 has now become a significant problem in terms of finding information but the solution is on the horizon with Web 3.0.

Web 3.0 the semantic web

The semantic or thinking web is in the development stage and if successful it will deliver an 'intelligent search' to cut through the Web

2.0 clutter and present the precise information we are seeking. Consider the literal size of the problem. No single authority is in charge of the internet so imagine a library where every day people walk in, place new books on the shelves, at random, but don't tell the librarian. On the Web each day an average of 128,000 new websites are added, 247 billion emails are sent (81% spam), 27.3 million tweets are posted, 70,000 new videos are uploaded to You Tube, 126 million blogs are updated and an average of 83.3 million photographs are added to Facebook. The Apple Apps store for the iphone and ipad now contains 350,000 Apps (mini programs on a wide range of topics) and on 22nd January 2011 a significant milestone was reached when the ten billionth App was downloaded. The App '*Paper Gilder*' was downloaded by Gail Davis of Orpinton in Kent, UK and she was awarded $10,000 by Apple to mark the event. However, Apple is registering exponential growth with the 25th billionth App due to be downloaded mid 2012. The sheer number of Apps is hard to comprehend - If you spent only a single minute looking at each one it would take 35 weeks of continuous 24/7 viewing to view all of them but as you viewed, thousands more would have been added. How about if you want to rent a holiday cottage in Italy? If you search using Google for '*holiday cottage Italy*' you will end up with 7,150,000 hits ranging from single individuals advertising their own holiday cottage to a commercial website with a database of hundreds of cottages to choose from. Many of us end up with search exhaustion. It is the digital equivalent of panning for gold as we sift and sift to find the nuggets and so it is no wonder that after a few hours many of us give up and walk into a high street travel agency and select a holiday package. It is possible to refine the search by using the advance search features employed by most search engines or by individual websites but this tends to only shave off a few thousand hits and does not resolve the central problem. Web 3.0 will use a combination of smart ontology based searches, avatars and voice recognition software to interface with the internet. Computers will move from being largely processing-centric to data-centric with the ability to sift large amounts of data to isolate the key information required. By 2020 we may find ourselves in the Star Trek world of *Computer, find me....* Voice recognition software and speaking computers already exist. If you use a Sat Nav in your car or booked a room over the telephone at Premierinn.com you will be listening to and/or speaking to a computer and have perhaps discovered how clear and realistic the voices can be. In both cases the computer is following a a delivery date etc. The challenge is to perfect software that can 'intelligently' draw each task from such complex sentences and successfully execute the tasks and preferably by voice command. The first steps in this direction appeared with the launch of the Apple iphone 4s in October 2011 with inbuilt voice command. Although in this case the voice is not called Oracle but Siri who introduces herself as your 'humble personal assistant'. Siri will respond to a question on the weather outside by specifying the weather forecast and chances of rain if I ask should I take an umbrella? I could ask Siri to wake me at 7.30 a.m. and the alarm is set without me having to take any further action or to play me a song by Adele etc. Siri also draws information from the Wolframalpha database and will answer most factually based questions like, what is the capital of Chile or what is £70 in dollars etc. A further significant step on the pathway to 'smart' ontology searches was the development in December 2011 of a program called 'summly' by sixteen year old Londoner Nick D'Aloiso to search and find not web hits but the precise information required. To paraphrase Bill Gates he is not frightened of competition from a corporate research department but the creativity of a young student. The interface will increasingly be the smartphone, rather than laptops or netbooks or even the ipad and similar tablets because they are highly portable and all connected to the internet via Wi-Fi or a 3G and increasingly 4G links. 91% of people in the UK now own a mobile phone and half of the new phones sold in 2011, some 3.3 million, were smartphones. The new generation of 3G and 4G mobile or cell telephones are converging with computers to give us pocket sized but highly powerful mobile computers with video call capability. The Motorola Atrix smartphone comes with the option of a standard laptop sized keyboard and screen which springs to life when the phone is docked to provide laptop functionality. In a similar way the Asus Padfone docks with a smartphone to provide full tablet large screen access. The phone in your pocket has more processing power than the computers of the 1.0 age and the explosion of apps offers endless capabilities. One of the most recent apps in development uses 'near field' technology to permit payments in a shop by waving a phone over a terminal in a very similar way to the use of pre-payment Oyster cards on the London underground. By 2015 we may all start to enter a truly cashless society. The Apple iphone is the well-known market leader selling 50 million phones in little over two years but others employing the new Google Android operating system are catching up fast. In the third quarter of 2010 80.9 million smartphones from the current 55,000 to 200,000. However, a further possibility is the transmission of a wifi signal over redundant TV channels following the switch over to digital TV. The wifi signal could be received by any wifi enabled laptop and computer across a whole city or region at vastly reduce costs. Currently many companies like Virgin are already advertising the 'superfast internet' with promised download speeds of 100mb as against the standard 2mb broadband download speed using 4g technology. The European Union has set a target for all homes to have access to 100mb broadband download speeds by 2020. However, this may be eclipsed by British Telecom (BT) who have announced plans for new Fibre to the Premises (FTTP) service with a promised download speed of 300 mb. At that sort of speed the hourglass or circular loading symbols on our computers will be history and whole films will download in three seconds. The DVD rental industry will switch online. We can also expect internet enabled televisions to become standard as consumers upgrade their televisions. The first combined TVi sets from Sony in collaboration with Google were unveiled September 2010 followed by Google January 2011 and Samsung May 2011. Internet enabled TVs will display the normal choice of TV channels but also search and find programmes or movies etc that you specify plus full access to the internet. The world's TV is online and services like *Streamdirecttv.com* will currently deliver to your computer or TVi 4,500 TV channels which is the combined output from 84 different countries including all 845 channels available in the USA, Australia 339, Canada 633 etc. However, no doubt we will still complain of repeats! Perhaps make your own goods at home? The Thing-O-Matic 3D printer uses liquid plastic instead of ink to lay down thin layers of plastic which instantly hardens to make physical 3D objects e.g. a cup. Experiments with a metal alloy are underway and with synthetic food and so within the next ten years you might select a product off the internet and download software to your printer to 'print' it. Also expect the spread of nano technology and advances in genetic profiling both of which will revolutionise diagnosis, health care and surgery, in particular, and significantly increase life expectancy. This will be aided by the ability, to grow in a laboratory, replacement body parts from your own cells. Already scientists can grow cartilage into noses, ears, heart values etc. The first windpipe was perfected in 2010 and major organs will follow. It will become common at birth to freeze stem cells to grow spare body parts as needed. In a related scientific breakthrough the creation of the world's first synthetic life was announced on 20th May 2010 by Dr. Craig Venter of the Venter Institute in the United States. Venter copied and altered the DNA sequence of the bacterium *Mycoplasma mycoides* to create the first bacterium not present in nature. The breakthrough holds the promise of microbes with artificially induced abilities to attack and kill cancer cells, to digest oil from oil spills, to create biofuels etc. Allied to this research is In-vitro cell growth or essentially synthetic meat production to replace the livestock down on the farm i.e. the ability to 'grow' real edible beef, chicken etc in vats from the relevant muscle cells. The 2010 Nobel prize for Physics was won by Professors Andre Geim and Konstantin Novoselov of Manchester University for their development of Graphene a revolutionary super-strong but light material. Graphene is a super-thin flexible layer of graphite carbons only one atom thick but 200 times stronger than steel. Three million sheets of graphene would only be 1mm thick and because of high electrical connectivity it could revolutionise all digital products in both size and shape. Human robots in the form of exoskeletons are already in development and will transfer super-strength to human arms and legs via a strap-on lightweight 'suit' and with the attachment of body armour revolutionise the battlefield and the lift capacity for construction workers, farmers etc. The same technology may permit the physically disabled to walk again. In terms of wider technology expect a much more automated society with the appearance of robots of all shapes and sizes to perform different tasks across the workplace and home. However, do not imagine the robots from the film irobot but rather 'intelligent' machines and appliances that anticipate requirements or react to commands and follow scripted actions. The 'Watson' supercomputer unveiled by IBM in February 2011 holds 200 million pages of data covering every conceivable topic and can speak answers to any question and significantly compare and contrast information and think about options before providing an answer. The leading U.S. expert on artificial intelligence has predicted that by 2030 such computers will match human intelligence and thereafter approach 'singularity' the ability to outthink the human brain and arrive at conclusions and advances beyond human abilities. You may have noticed the slow but significant spread of self-checkouts across our supermarkets and retailers but be prepared for robot operators who will greet, scan goods, accept your electronic payment and wish you a good day. The public concerns might be eased by a future of thorium based nuclear reactors rather than uranium based. Thorium is up to 10,000 times less radioactive than uranium, more abundant and does not produce any weapons grade plutonium. Finally, 'printed electronics' will allow computer circuitry to be printed onto textiles, cardboard, metal, paper and result in 'clever' colour, sound and text altering applications for packaging, billboards, signs, clothes etc.

High level skill demands

All of the above rapid advances in technology are highlighted because they raise the possibility of whole new fields of employment with developments and applications mushrooming every five years. The 21st century workforce, as quoted by Toffler as quoted by Toffler in Chapter One, will need, 'the ability to learn, unlearn and relearn' to keep pace. Many new jobs will be created and most will be high skilled jobs across all of the above high tech fields raising a demand for more employees with STEM related qualifications (Science, Technology, Engineering and Maths). The most promising hi-tech fields for future employment are: aerospace, silicon electronics, plastics and printed electronics, industrial biotechnologies, composite materials and nano technology. Western economies have lost manufacturing employment to the low wage economies of the East and Far East and our future prosperity will rest on developing hi-tech industries, the knowledge based Service Sector and an expansion of self-employment as those with a craft, or a specialist knowledge or skill create virtual companies and sell their goods or services worldwide via the internet. A series of short videos have been posted, by some very creative people, on You Tube www.youtube.com to chart the emergence of the global economy. Enter the search terms, *'Now you know'* or *'Shift happens'* or even *'Web 4.0'* and you can absorb the scale and pace of the global economic and technological revolution. By the simple act of accessing and watching the videos you will have entered the *Knowledge Age* and if you post a comment or even create and post your own short video you will be part of Web 2.0 if not the Web 3.0 world. This hi-tech world of employment is the employment market our children and students will enter 2020+ and our schools and colleges need to deliver the relevant skills and qualifications. Teach for the future not the past.

3 The i-generations

"You are a Timex watch in a digital age."
A rebuke to the character John McClane in the film Diehard 4.0[1]

The i-generation or Generation Y were born circa 1980 and they are familiar and comfortable with most aspects of information technology. The i-generation has attracted many studies and many descriptive labels e.g. Googlers, Millenniums, Digital Natives because their norms essentially presage a different future. The future rests in the letter i. The i prefix could be for internet or information or individual or even interactive although some sociologists might argue, immure. However, in terms of the development of future learning the i is firmly for independent and the rise of the *independent learner*. We are all watching a significant revolution as the new rather than the older generation become the seers and the guides to the future as they revolutionise the way we find, access, view and present information. It is notable that the dominant names and products of the Web 2.0 era e.g. Microsoft, Apple, Dell, Google, and Facebook emerged not from some corporate research department after many years of research but from the creativity of individual young students. Bill Gates was 13 when he first dabbled in computers, the late Steve Jobs (1955-2011) was 16, Michael Dell was 19 and Mark Zuckerberg was 20 and a student at Harvard University when he first hit upon the idea of creating an electronic version of the university 'facebook' of students' pen portraits. The rest is recent history and Zuckerberg at age 24 is currently the world's youngest billionaire with an estimated wealth of $4billion. However, he is far from the wealthiest entrepreneur as indicated by Figure 1 below. Within the UK in 2010 the number one company in The Times list of 100 highest performing technology companies was the game company PKR established by Jez San. San was only 16 in 1982 when he started his first company Argonaut to sell computer games. More recently in 2008 Ethan Nicholas wrote the game *ishoot* as an 'App' for the Apple iphone and to date he has made over $1 million from downloads with a peak of 17,000 downloads in a single day. Writing an App for the Apple iphone or ipad is the Y generation version of the goldrush. The latest iphone game success is *Bubble Ball* released January 2011 and written by self-taught 14 year old Robert Nay from Utah. Bubble Ball has been downloaded over two million times and overtaken Angry Birds in the Apps download chart. How did he discover how to write an App? He googled it! Nor is it just the younger generation who are discovering that creativity can pay. Thirty-six year old Iain Dodsworth was unemployed in 2007 when he wrote ' Tweetdeck' essentially a home page to manage social networking contacts. Tweetdeck was sold to Twitter in May 2011 for £25 million. Creative industries are the wealth creators of tomorrow and so it is perhaps not too surprising that a re-evaluation of Bloom's cognitive taxonomy has identified 'creativity' as the highest order of cognitive development. Perhaps the most creative of all are the following top ten who turned a simple internet idea or concept into significant wealth creation for themselves but also creating significant employment for others.

Figure 1

The i-generation rich list			
Rank	Name	Company	$Billion
1	Larry Page	Google	19.8
2	Sergey Brin	Google	19.8
3	Jeff Bezos	Amazon	18.1
4	Mark Zuckerberg	Facebook	4.0
5	Eric Schmidt	Google	7.0
6	Pierre Omidyar	Ebay	6.7
7	Mark Cuban	Broadcast	2.5
8	Peter Thiel	Paypal	1.5
9	David Filo	Yahoo	1.16
10	Jerry Yang	Yahoo	1.15

Forbes Internet billionaires 2011[2]

However, the above are far from the richest people in the world and the old world of finance, steel and property can also generate significant fortunes. The richest person in the world according to Forbes 2011 is Carlos Slim Helu of Mexico with a fortune of $74 billion garnered from telecoms followed in second place by Bill Gates of Microsoft with $56 billion and in third place Warren Buffett with $50 billion from finance and banking.

Generation Z

Generation Y bridge the pre and post internet generations but are you ready for Generation Z? Generation Z were born 2000+ and the first cohort will be in your high school classroom in September 2011 and college classroom in September 2016. They are the first fully fledged i-generation who know nothing of life before the internet, X Box, PS2, Wii, multiple TV channels, mobile/cell phone, ipod, digital cameras, blogs, RSS feeds, Google, You Tube, Amazon, Facebook, Twitter, netbooks, tablets etc. By the time they reach college in 2016 the ipad2 (3) and perhaps (4) and similar tablets will be commonplace and mobile computing will be the norm. Generation Z will naturally Google any question (or perhaps Bing) and they are by instinct independent but also significantly, for future learning, collaborative learners. Web 2.0 and the emerging Web 3.0 emphasise interaction and interconnectivity to the extent that the i-generation, both Y and Z, largely ignore terrestrial television. Sitting on the sofa passively watching a mainstream TV channel is a Generation X activity. The i-generation are not sitting on the sofa. They are on the internet speaking to friends via Skype, reading a blog, perhaps adding to their own blog, updating their Facebook profile, making a video with friends to post on Youtube, downloading music, shopping online or selling something on Ebay etc. If you don't know your generation then consider the dominant music technology when you were a teenager:

- Baby-boomer 1940-59 Vinyl
- Generation X 1960-79 Tape
- Generation Y 1980-1999 CD/Walkman
- Generation Z 2000-2019 ipod /cloud streaming
- Generation Alpha 2020-2039 ?

The above boundaries have soft edges because technology overlaps in relation to early and late adopters as the different generations commix.

38

The online teen

A snapshot and insight into the extent of this online world was provided by William Murray aged 15 from Chelmsford, Essex, UK who recorded how he spent Saturday 26th September 2009 as part of The Times, 'newspaper Day in a life of...' series.

Between breakfast and lunch he:

- Checked and replied to emails,
- Checked the weather forecast online
- Surfed comparison websites to find the best price for a computer game
- Updated his Facebook profile,
- Posted new photographs,
- Chatted to friends on MSM
- Chatted to friends returning from a school trip to France via a webcam
- Listened to music over the internet via Spotify
- Watched a DVD
- Checked the balance of his online bank account
- Started an English assignment

After lunch and through into the early evening he:

- Listened to chill-out music from Spotify
- Downloaded some software for his Xbox
- Finished his English assignment and copied it to a memory stick
- Played a game on Xbox
- Viewed latest video releases on You Tube
- Chatted to friends on MSM
- Watched Sky News
- Sat out in the sunshine and listened to music on his iphone
- Chatted to friends using Skype
- Downloaded and watched an episode of NCIS
- Watched a recording of X Factor
- Updated his Facebook status

In the late evening through to lights out at 10.40 p.m. he:

- Looked at photographs taken by his friends on their French trip
- Chatted to friends via the Webcam
- Watched, the TV show 'Mock the Week'.
- Added a commentary to his new photograph file on Facebook
- Set the alarm on his iphone

William makes regular and wide use of technology throughout the day. Whereas a generation ago most teenagers passively watched whatever was on television or complained of boredom (remember those long empty Sundays?) , William has choices and he interacts, contributes and creates. Although he largely remains in his bedroom to use the internet William is not socially isolated. He is in regular communication with his friends via social networking and via his mobile/cell and engages in rich interactions with them. Generation X also used to regularly escape to their bedrooms and so escaping from parents is not a new phenomenon. Teenagers have always confided in friends first and parents second. However, the family generations collide when the i-generation insist upon attaching Wii or Kinect to the TV and persuading Generation X off the sofa to play an electronic sport or to engage in energetic disco dancing. The TVi or internet enabled TV will dominate TV sales 2012+ and place the internet at the heart of the home. Once the internet is positioned in the centre of the family living room the oft repeated concerns about teenage social isolation will evaporate as families explore entertainment choices and engage in joint activities. The whole family will be able to surf and consider holiday options, view products and shop online, enjoy a You tube video, look at a live webcam, download a book, play a music video, look at the family photo album, enjoy sport, view a movie, play a game etc. In addition once Tablets and Smartphones become widespread with the ability to connect to the internet anytime and anyplace William will leave his bedroom more often. Finally, when William applies for a job he'll probably not bother with completing a standard CV but will post a short video presentation of himself and his interests and abilities on You Tube for employers to view.

Online activity

The British Office of Communications (Ofcom.org.uk), monitors and regulates the UK media industry and published its seventh annual survey of UK media activity in August 2010[3]. The report provided a comprehensive breakdown of the extent and breadth of all UK media consumption. In 2010 76% of British homes owned a computer with 73% connected to the internet and 71% enjoying a broadband connection. However when analysed by social class 88% of the higher income A-B homes enjoyed internet access compared to 54% of low income D-E homes. In total nine million adults do not own a computer but poverty is not the only possible reason - age and interest are also significant factors. 39% of non-computer owners are over 65 years and when questioned as to why they did not own a computer the common reply was *'see no need for one'*, rather than cost. Only 13% of the low income D-E families without an internet connection specified cost as their reason. It would appear that the majority of people without an internet connection simply do not see a need for one. The TV personality Vanessa Fletz, for instance, is proud of the fact that she does not own a computer and has boasted that she has never sent a single email. There are also tales of Generation X managers in many businesses who ask their personal assistants to print off all their emails. In 2010 the average Briton spent 7 hours 5 minutes of their (average) 15 hours 45 minutes awake time (equivalent to 45%) consuming media. The key trends in UK media consumption were reported as follows:

- Nearly half of UK citizens' awake time (45%) is spent engaging with media
- The significant majority (90%) own a mobile/cell phone
- For Generation Y mobile/cell phone are replacing the use of landlines. 15% of households do not have a landline and rely upon their mobile.
- Texting is the primary use of mobile phones – 100 billion texts were sent in 2009 equivalent to 1700 for every person in the UK.
- Print whether newspapers and books etc is in decline and largely consumed by those over 45 and increasingly the 55+ age-groups
- Most broadband connections are Wifi to permit multiple access across the home

- Laptops are replacing desktop computers and ending the need for dedicated computer desks and/or study corners in our homes.
- Mobile broadband is increasing with 32% using their mobile/cell phone to access the internet.
- Mass audiences for TV are in sharp decline as TV competes against other media choices for our attention. Only 36% of young people say they would miss TV.
- Selecting what and when to watch TV programmes is accelerating via catch-up services like BBC iplayer.
- Email is the dominant computer function at 86% of computer activity followed by general surfing the internet at 84%

OECD survey of internet usage

In 2010 the Organisation for Economic Co-operation and Development (OECD) published extensive research on access to and the use made of computers and the internet by fifteen year old pupils across its 65 member nations. Overall less than 1% of fifteen year old pupils had no access to a computer at home. Figure Two shows the top ten countries with the highest level of home internet access[4]:

Figure 2

Country	% home internet
Iceland	97.7
Sweden	96.7
Korea	96.5
Netherlands	96.5
Denmark	95.7
Norway	95.6
Canada	94
Switzerland	93.4
Finland	92.6
United Kingdom	90.4

The lowest rate of home internet access was Mexico with only 23.3% of pupils connected. In terms of internet usage, 'the majority of 15 year-olds use their computers more frequently at home than at school. In most OECD countries more than 80% use computers at home several times a *week'.* [5] This may reflect completion of homeworks or simply more time and fewer distractions to conduct research. Undertaking research was second in the list of online activities as listed:

Chatting online 69%
Research 61%
Email 60%
Playing games 58%
Downloading music 50%
Downloading software 41%
Collaborating with others 37%.

Access to a computer (as opposed to internet) at home for schoolwork confers a learning advantage and there is a notable gap in terms of access between low income and high income households. As the table indicates Sweden tops the poll with 99.9% of high income families having a home computer but this is only 3% above the OECD average of 96.7%. A computer is essentially a norm in most high income households compared to the OECD average of 72.4% for low income households as identified in Figure Three[6].

Figure 3

Country	High income	Low income
Sweden	99.9%	94.2%
United Kingdom	99.8%	86.4%
United States	99.5%	69.5%
OECD average	96.7%	72.4%

Interestingly the data shows a strong correlation between homes that invested in books to help with homework and homes with a computer. Consequently the key issue is not so much socio-economic status but to what extent learning is encouraged and supported within the home. The most significant correlation with achievement is the effort invested and the qualification level of the parent(s) or guardian(s) and in particular the mother. It is a reminder that initiatives to promote parental involvement and how to support and promote learning at home are important and can make a significant difference to progress at college level as well as school. The provision of online resources, newsletters and Virtual Learning Environment (VLE) links for parents may significantly assist this involvement.

Online children

Children tend to embrace new technology more quickly than adults because it is their norm. A BBC Television survey of 24,000 children aged 11-16 in March 2011 revealed the following access to technology[7]:

- 95 % had access to a home computer with internet access
- 1.7% had a home computer but no internet access
- 62% had a games console with internet access
- 26.5% had a games console but no internet access
- 60% coached older family members in using new technology
- 67% had a mobile /cell phone with internet access (56% for eleven year olds)
- 26.7% had a mobile / cell phone without internet access

In addition, the children preferred to communicate by text message (70.3%), and social networking sites (66.6%) and talking on their mobiles (49.6%). Email is falling significantly as a medium with only 12.2% of the rising generation using it to communicate. These trends reinforce the need for schools and colleges to embrace texting via smartphones. In terms of aspirations by age 30 Generation Z are little different to any other generation and despite the often stated concern of a focus on fame this comes at the bottom of their list of interests as highlighted in Figure 4:

Figure 4 Children's aspirations by age 30

Aspiration	%
Owning a house	34.9
Earning a lot	31.1
Married	25.5
Happiness	23.6
Worthwhile job	20.2
Children	18.5
Good car	10.5
Personal achievement	7.6
Fame	7.2
I don't know	1.8
Other	5.2

Generation Z express a very normal range of aspirations with over half 57% expressing a desire to go to university. It is likely that most will not depart too far from the Mr and Mrs Average UK citizen profile in Figure 5 as published by the Office for National Statistics May 2011[8].

Figure 5

Profile of Mr and Mrs Average Citizen 2011		
Aspect	Male	Female
Lifespan	79 years	82 years
Qualifications	A-Level / Level 3	GCSE / Level 2
Salary	£28,270	£22,151
Age married	31	29
Height	5' 9"	5'3"
Weight	13 St	11St

Multi-tasking

Against the average media consumption of 7 hours 5 minutes the age-group 16-24 consume 9 hours 32 minutes worth of media per day but due to multi-viewing/listening this is compressed into 6 hours 32 minutes. As the i-generation watch a DVD they may also be completing a purchase on the internet or texting a friend or downloading music. They may also regularly view two or three TV channels at the same time without fully settling to watch a whole programme or movie. Students at Kansas State University in the United States posted a video on You Tube in 2008 entitled, '*A vision of students today*' and confirmed a preference for multitasking. The Kansas students claimed an average 26.5 hour day as listed in Figure 6:[9]

Figure 6

Activity	Hours
Online	3.5
Part-time job	2
Study	3
Watch TV	1.5
Listen to music	2.5
Use cell/mobile	2
eating	2
Attend lessons	3
sleep	7
Total activity	**26.5**

The above pattern of activity reflects the UK survey data and has led to popular concerns that too much multi-tasking may lead to low attention spans and ultimately underachievement. At the same time in the UK GCSE and A-Level achievement rates are rising year on year. The i-generation multi-task or more correctly 'parallel process' simply because they can. They have entertainment and communication options that did not exist even five years ago. It is also a misnomer to assume that only the i-generation multitask. Generation X will happily read a newspaper, book or magazine while also watching TV or listening to the radio or to music. We must guard against assumptions that a particular lifestyle is harmful or less beneficial. Prior to the alarm over the 'dangers' of multi-tasking generating low attention spans the popular concern was the 'dangers' of inactive 'couch potatoes' sprawled in front of their TV sets. The alarmist articles about low attention spans tend to reflect the cultural primacy afforded to (printed) books. A survey by the UK charity Booktrust, in 2009, revealed that the average British child owned 75 books but many more DVDs and computer games. The unspoken subtext was that learning was in decline. Our deep bond with books and their association with learning is over 500 years old. Johannes Gutenberg invented the printing press circa 1439 and by 1500 books shifted into mass production across Europe in the world's first information revolution. Prior to Gutenberg information and learning was primarily oral and conveyed by lecture, speeches and stories but also experiential via display, demonstrations, observation, diagrams, models, art, sketching, collecting, cataloguing, and experimenting. No doubt many at the time questioned the loss of personal investigation and individual activity as opposed to the passive activity of reading a book. However, the book made information readily accessible and established a shared and authoritative knowledge base that significantly advanced learning and ushered in the Enlightenment. In Europe the ruling classes added impressive libraries to their mansions. However, how far were all of our book owning monarchs, aristocrats and landed gentry intelligent, knowledgeable and wise? Books, by themselves, do not instantly confer learning any more than the possession of a computer. Both are windows to learning and we must avoid the assumption that the only worthwhile learning or information arises from (printed) books. It must be remembered that books are not disappearing but are merely in transition from print to electronic form. When Generation X were children their parents berated them for watching too much television, reading too many 'silly' comics and listening to too much pop music with the 'nonsensical', *yeah, yeah, yeah* lyrics.

Generational differences in media usage 2010

The following collation of Ofcom data 2010[10] in Figure Seven provides an overview of the generational technology gap between the i-generation and generation X (circa 1960). The majority of teachers are Generation X and the majority of students are Generation Y although Generation Y teachers are entering our staffrooms in increasing numbers.

Figure 7

Aspect	i-generations Y&Z	Generation X
Telephone	Primarily mobile/cell and upgrading to smartphone	Primarily landline
Telephone usage	Prefer texting over voice. Texting forms 30% of their total media activity.	Prefer voice over texting. Texting is only 6% of their total media activity.
Computer communication	Via Facebook or instant messaging services	Via email
Computer use	Social networking and entertainment plus 40% of 15-24 year olds watch TV online.	Finding information and functional purchases of train tickets, holidays etc. Only 21% watch TV online.
Music	Digital downloads to ipod or mobile/cell or streaming from Spotify or similar	Primarily CD players
Television use	Largely use TV to watch DVDS, music channel, news channel and this accounts for 26% of their total media consumption.	Largely watch scheduled programmes like news at 6 p.m. etc and this accounts for 51% of their total media consumption.
Recorded TV	77% select programmes from iplayer /You Tube or similar on their computer or Xbox/Playstation.	42% select programmes from iplayer /You Tube or similar on their computer or Xbox/Playstation.
Radio	Preference is listening via laptop /phone and accounts for 9 % of their total media activity. Only 4% listen to a radio.	Preference is listening via a radio and accounts for 14% of their total media activity. Only 2% access radio via laptop/phone.

Aspect	i-generations Y&Z	Generation X
Games	55% on average play skills based games and often competitive with other players online and accounts for 5% of their total media activity.	22% on average play electronic games and this accounts for 1% of their total media activity.
Print	Reading books, magazines or newspapers accounts for 3% of their total media activity.	Reading books, magazines and newspaper accounts for 10 % of their total media activity.
Uploading	74% have uploaded photos to the Web, 51% contributed to a blog and 26% made and posted a video.	38% have uploaded photos to the Web, 15% contributed to a blog and 5% made and posted a video.
Social networking	77% maintain a profile on social networking websites like Facebook.	30% maintain a profile on social networking websites like Facebook.
Personal website	26% have set up and maintain their own website	12% have set up and maintain their own website
Write a blog	22% write and publish their own blog	5% write and publish their own blog
Voice over Internet Protocol (VOIP)	16% on average use services like Skype to have video and voice contact with friends and family.	5% on average use services like Skype to have video and voice contact with friends and family.

The data illustrates that the i-generation have adopted Web 2.0 technology at levels at least twice that of Generation X. However, perhaps different social priorities are at work? The i-generation and young adults largely use Web 2.0 technology to build and maintain social relationships and friendships. Generation X are much more likely to be in settled relationships with periodic, rather than daily, contact with friends and wider family. Similarly, the online activities of Generation Z reflect their interests and consequently care must be taken not to pillory Generation X for being behind the times. Generation X will use and do use information technology once they see a particular benefit e.g. one of the highest adoption rates of new technology by Generation X is watching TV online via a catch-up service like BBC iplayer which was launched December 2007. Across the age-group 35+ 73% watch programmes online which is not far behind the 77% of 15-34 year olds who watch online. In terms of e-readers 6% of over 55s have purchased an e-reader compared to 5% of 18-24 year olds according to a *Silver Poll* published in March 2011[11]. The poll revealed that the Amazon Kindle has claimed 47% of sales followed by the Apple ipad 31% and Sony e-reader at 14% of sales. Many members of Generation X have also mastered and discovered the joys of Skype to keep in touch with distant family members. Generation X tend to be more functionally inclined rather than general browsers and the early adopters of electronic media. They have also, as Toffler' might say had to 'unlearn' older technology and deserve credit for 'distance travelled' in terms of adopting and applying new technology.

Generation X technology

Generation X teachers circa 1980 will remember:

- Manual typewriters for typing letters and handouts
- Inserting carbon paper between two sheets of typing paper to create a 'carbon copy' of any letter or memo for the file or to copy to a third person. Interestingly the CC abbreviation has crossed over into the digital era as our emails have a CC entry to copy the email to a third person. This is not a Latin abbreviation, as many might suspect, but simply the now misplaced term carbon copy (CC).
- Tippex fluid to paint over and correct any typing mistakes
- Using a memo pad to write memos - post and wait 3-4 days for the recipient to send a reply.
- Lots of paperclips to attach notes to memos and other printed material for circulation to others (Post It notes had not been invented).
- Using Letraset to create labels by ruling a straight pencil line and carefully pressing each individual letter onto the paper.
- The Banda machine to print handouts (first type your handout onto a waxed paper Banda master. Attach the Banda master to the rotating drum of the Banda machine and then turn the handle to print each copy of the handout. Most teachers had purple fingers from the dye used and impressive arm muscles!
- Adding images to handouts by finding an appropriate cutting from a newspaper or magazine. Sticking the cutting into place and then applying lots of Tippex fluid around the borders otherwise a visible line appeared when photocopied.

- Chalk and black boards and lots of chalk dust over clothes
- Large reel to reel film projectors with educational films hired from suppliers like the Rank Organisation and delivered by courier
- Cassette tape recorders for playing music and voice recording
- Film strip projectors (a strip of film negatives that were threaded into a small projector and projected slide by slide and likewise for slide projectors).
- To shoot a video first book a large video camera on a tripod and a technician
- To play a video book the sole machine for your department, well in advance, and push into your classroom
- To take a photograph first book the sole department camera, purchase a film on petty cash, take the photographs and leave with a chemist shop to be developed into pre-specified print sizes.
- To display images first copy the image or text onto a clear acetate sheet and project onto a white screen using an Over Head Projector (OHP).
- To contact a colleague ring their staffroom on the internal telephone and more often than not dictate a message to be left on their desk.
- To research a topic visit the library and search relevant reference books and or encyclopaedias. Find any useful books on the shelves. Use micro-fiche files on a reader to search archived information and borrow books not in your library stock via interlibrary loan – wait at least a week if not two to receive the book(s).
- Finally to ensure you had money in your pocket for the weekend nip out between lessons to the bank, queue up and hand over a cheque made out to 'cash'.

It is often a tempting to question the benefits of computers but most of us would accept that computer technology has improved all aspects of the above 1980s technology. However, the improvements are largely in terms of upgrading classroom equipment and classroom support with electronic alternatives. Powerpoint may have replaced the OHP but how we teach and learn has not significantly altered. This is not the fault of the technology yet it is interesting how many worthy reports highlight that investment in IT has not produced a noticeable leap forward in learning or in exam pass rates. Nor will a brand new school building. It is what happens in it and how technology is used that will improve learning. Despite significant investment in IT the technology remains a clumsy 'bolt-on' rather than embedded activity and the dominant pedagogy remains a teacher talking at the front of a classroom with largely passive learners taking notes. Learners either grasp a topic within the short timetabled window of opportunity (the lesson) or they don't. However, a Virtual Learning Environment (VLE) can offer a repeat of the lesson material, additional support materials, recommended internet sites, peer forums, blogs, video, email support and exemplars. This is natural territory for Generation Z who already confidently navigate cross all electronic media and as young as three years can navigate the internet. Is your school or college VLE a live learning environment or a rarely visited repository for random files?

Generation Z internet use

The first cohort of Generation Z (born 2000) entered High School in September 2011. They are reputed to be more independent and community orientated than Generation Y with less focus on the conspicuous consumption of the 'right brands' and a 'my rights...' mindset. They express a 'one world' or 'connected world' perspective in terms of climate change, sustainability, fair trade and green issues in general and question inequality and instinctively seek to share, collaborate and promote equality. Generation Z have the same hopes and fears as previous generations but significantly for them computer technology is an absolute norm. Visit Toys R Us or a similar toy shop and look at the wide range of electronic media available to infants and 'teentronics' for the older children. They can select from simplified but powerful digital cameras, MP3 players, DVD players, laptops, music centres, e-story readers, hand held game machines, mobile phones, karaoke machines, dance machines and game consoles. The downside is the scale and overt nature of the gender stereotyping with the girls' products all packaged in shades of pink and the boys in dark greens and blacks and with associated 'soft, caring' or 'hard, aggressive' imagery. By the simple act of browsing and buying electronic media (and other toys) children very much absorb the nursery rhyme message that little girls are made of *'sugar and spice'* and that little boys are made of, *'snails and puppy dogs' tails'*.

That is perhaps a battle for another time. *Leapfrog.com* offer simulated laptops and tablets for children from age two albeit with basic push button functions but the concept of self-access learning and even Apps is being established at a very young age. The associated selection of software, books, games encompass most aspects of reading, writing, numeracy, drawing and music as well as thinking and logic based puzzles and games. The use by very young children of computers and the internet is unremarked and unremarkable. This is apparent from the following data in Figure 8 compiled from a survey of 5,000 American children aged 6-11 in 2007.[13]

Figure 8

Kids' online activities 2007 (Among kids ages 6-11 who went online in the last 30 days			
Online activity	All kids %	Boys %	Girls %
Played online games	78.1	77.7	78.5
Did stuff for homework	34.2	32.8	35.5
Listened to music	28.6	24.1	33.0
Watched videos	26.2	28.9	23.5
Looked for websites/Surfed the web	22.7	21.1	24.2
Used email	20.4	15.8	24.8
Found out about different things I like	15.7	16.0	15.3
Got tips or cheats on games	15.6	25.8	5.6
Shopped or looked at things to buy	13.1	14.1	12.1
Downloaded music	12.7	12.0	13.4
Downloaded games	11.8	13.7	10.0
Used instant messenger	9.3	6.6	11.9
Went to chat rooms	3.7	3.1	4.2
Have their own email address	29.2	26.3	32.0

The top activity, by far, for both girls and boys is playing games with interestingly the girls recording a marginally higher level of playing games than the boys. The gender stereotyping referred to earlier is also sharply present across the choice of games offered to young girls and boys with the boys tending to select highly competitive adventure and 'chase' games. This is further reinforced by the higher interest shown by boys in finding 'cheats' and related game downloads because they are seeking an advantage to allow them to

52

leap through the game levels. The girls make greater use of social networking e.g. email, instant messenger and chatrooms for communication with friends and also have a greater interest in music. In terms of wider communication over a quarter of the boys and girls have their own email address but overall teachers will be pleased to note that the second highest online activity within American data is completing homeworks. In the UK similar findings emerged from a survey conducted by the BBC in association with the Open University (www.openlearn.net). The Child of our Times survey[14] tracks the development of a representative sample of children born in 2000. In contrast to the often alarmist headlines of young children watching too much TV or being addicted to computer technology we discover that at age 10 playing outside and playing with toys remain the dominant childhood interests as listed in Figure 9:

Figure 9

BBC Child of our times survey 2010 Time spent in different activities	
Activity	**Average minutes per day**
Playing outside	118
Playing with toys	118
Watching TV	67
Listening to music	31
Being read to	23
Writing	21
Watching a video/DVD	18
Reading	16
Using a computer	7
Playing video games	6

The above survey was conducted during the summer months when outdoor play might be expected to be high but clearly active play is still the dominant activity in children's lives. This was also reflected in TV viewing habits because the survey revealed that few of the children sat still and passively watched TV but engaged in a wide range of simultaneous activities. The data also shows that the use of a computer and playing video games is low down the rank order in comparison to all other activities and particularly with the time spent reading and writing. Consequently the dire alarmist predictions from some authors and commentators in relation to too much time spent on computers may be misplaced and perhaps more to do with headlines to fill and books to sell. The above data has been reinforced by a further survey of the lifestyles of 1000 children aged 5-16 conducted by Opinion Matters in the UK April, 2011.[15] The survey invited children to identify what made them happy. The activities with the highest responses were: 'playing with friends 83.7% followed by 'my birthday' 82.3% and 'spending time with my family' 79.6% . The electronic world first appeared in the rank order at a mid point with 'playing computer games' mentioned by 64% of respondents and lower down the rank order 'texting on a phone' 27.8% and 'using social networking sites' 20.9%. However as in the previous data the gender difference is notable In terms of playing computer games 71.9% of boys said this made them happy compared to 58.3% of girls but in terms of texting on a phone girls dominated with 32.2% enjoying texting compared to 21.7% of boys.

Creative excuses

A further survey of 1000 teachers by the online retailer *Pixmania.com*[16] in 2008 revealed that 68% of pupils wordprocess their homework and that the top five excuses for not completing homeworks were:

- My computer crashed and I lost it
- I finished my homework but then deleted it by accident
- I could not print it out
- My internet was down so I could not do any research
- I lost my laptop

Some children also offered more imaginative excuses:

- The Russians hacked into my dad's computer and stole my homework
- A burglar stole my printed-out homework along with the computer
- The PC exploded when our dog went to the toilet on it'.

This all makes for a refreshing change from, *my dog ate it* ! Overall Generation Z like any generation accept the world as they find it and their Web 2.0 world involves instant communication, instant information, regular choices, decisions, opinions, co-operation, competitions and problem solving. They operate interactive whiteboards as a norm and if confronted with an OHP machine they are baffled by the fact that it is not touch screen and there is nowhere to insert a memory stick. Generation Z have no preconceptions, no awareness of the speed or scale of the electronic revolution and no hesitation in adopting and using any form of electronic media. They will drive change in our High School and College classrooms. Are you ready for Generation Z?

Re-thinking the curriculum

"Strive for perfection in everything that you do. Take the best that exists and make it better. When it does not exist, design it.[1]

Henry Royce

Re-thinking the curriculum in terms of not only what we teach but also the balance between knowledge and skills is not a choice but a survival strategy within the 21st century global economy. The significant imperatives for change are:

- The sharp decline in unskilled and semi-skilled manufacturing employment,
- The growth of hi-technology solutions, applications and new products,
- The sharp rise in graduate level service sector employment,
- The demand for high personal and employability skills across low level as well as high level service sector employment,
- Online anyplace, anytime trading, living and working,
- Low cost, low risk self-employment opportunities,
- Global competition for contracts,
- The rise of the internet as 'Oracle' for learning and information.

The rising i-generations Y and Z have entered and will enter a much more technological society across all aspects of life and work and operate within a highly interconnected world. They will trade and compete for business within a global economy. The young person our children might compete against for future employment may be living in Shanghai or Mumbai. The related rising demand for high quality education has led many European and U.S. universities to open overseas campuses. The latest trend emerging in China, India, Middle East, Germany, Finland, France and South Korea is for whole degree courses to be taught in English so that the graduates emerge not just with their specialist degree knowledge but also, almost as an adjunct, fluent English. Qatar has invested in an 'Education city' on the outskirts of the capital Doha and so far six U.S., one French and one

British university have opened international campuses. Global education is becoming as much a reality as a global economy. Nor is the global economy mere hype. Visit *Peopleperhour.com* and discover a world-wide marketplace of business skills providers bidding for contracts. This is one of many similar websites. To win jobs and to ensure future prosperity it is important than our education system can deliver the high skills and qualifications needed by the rising hi-tech and established service sectors as traditional industries decline. We need to prosper from new products, share new markets and stay at the edge of new technological developments and this raises a demand for effective interpersonal and intrapersonal skills and creativity in bringing new products to market and adding value. The 21st Century service sector is 'people facing' and technology orientated at all levels and this is a very different working environment to the low skilled factory employment of the 20th Century. Even low qualified employment within the service sector demands relatively high skills in terms of effective people and IT skills. Our curriculum and pedagogy need to evolve with the balance between knowledge and skills tilted more firmly towards skills or to use the analogy of quiz shows more *Cube* than *Mastermind*. The mastery and recall of a specified set of facts that the latter tested might be impressive but it is the application of knowledge and the creative problem solving capabilities of the former that will drive the 21st century economy. Overall a strong consensus has emerged across the World's developed economies that future prosperity rests upon well-educated, digitally skilled and creative workforces. Curriculum planners worldwide are re-thinking their curriculum offers to place skills at the centre and, as far as possible, to foster in young people a deep sense of self-worth and (world) citizenship coupled with high interpersonal and intrapersonal skills. Individuals who first value themselves, will value other people and wider society. As Toffler has stated, *"the illiterate of the 21st Century will not be those who cannot read and write but those who cannot learn, unlearn and relearn"*.

The scale of the challenge

Our 20th Century curriculum was predicated on a tripartite system which sifted each cohort for those suitable for progression to university, skilled trades or in the case of the significant majority of school pupils into low skilled or unskilled labour. This 'ability pyramid' reflected the labour requirements of the 20th century with an industrial economy dominated by large scale unskilled or semi-skilled manufacturing employment and a small, graduate entry, professional skills sector. However, the service sector dominated economy of the 21st Century requires a more highly qualified workforce as illustrated by the following top 20 areas for rising and falling UK employment 2000-2010.

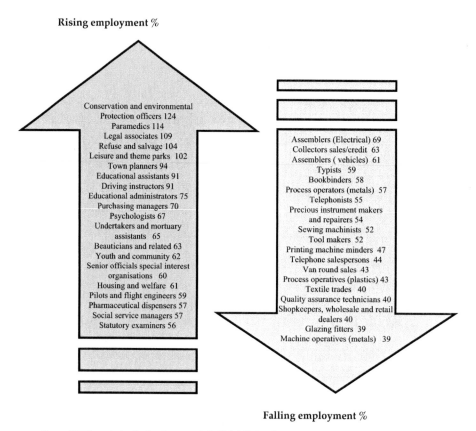

Rising employment %

Conservation and environmental Protection officers 124
Paramedics 114
Legal associates 109
Refuse and salvage 104
Leisure and theme parks 102
Town planners 94
Educational assistants 91
Driving instructors 91
Educational administrators 75
Purchasing managers 70
Psychologists 67
Undertakers and mortuary assistants 65
Beauticians and related 63
Youth and community 62
Senior officials special interest organisations 60
Housing and welfare 61
Pilots and flight engineers 59
Pharmaceutical dispensers 57
Social service managers 57
Statutory examiners 56

Assemblers (Electrical) 69
Collectors sales/credit 63
Assemblers (vehicles) 61
Typists 59
Bookbinders 58
Process operators (metals) 57
Telephonists 55
Precious instrument makers and repairers 54
Sewing machinists 52
Tool makers 52
Printing machine minders 47
Telephone salespersons 44
Van round sales 43
Process operatives (plastics) 43
Textile trades 40
Quality assurance technicians 40
Shopkeepers, wholesale and retail dealers 40
Glazing fitters 39
Machine operatives (metals) 39

Falling employment %

Source: UK Commission for Employment skills (UKCES) 2010.[2]

The above figures are percentages in terms of percentage increases or decreases in employment opportunities across the decade 2000-10. The rising areas of employment reflect the burgeoning service sector with most jobs requiring degree level qualifications whereas the falling areas of employment most often required semi-skilled or unskilled qualifications. The upward pressure on qualifications is highlighted by the following predictions for qualification requirements by 2020 by the UK Commission for Employment skills (UKCES).[3]

UK workforce qualifications 2008 and projected change 2020

Level	2008 %	2020 %
4	31	42
3	20	19
2	20	20
1	17	14
0	12	5

The levels relate to graduate level (Level 4), A-Level or Diploma (Level 3), GCSE or equivalent (Level 2) and Foundation qualifications (Level 1). The graduate entry market is expected to rise from 31% to 42% and within this pool employers are increasingly specifying a minimum requirement for a 2.1 degree classification. Those who achieve a 2.2 or 3rd class degree may find it increasingly difficult to find suitable employment. At the other end of the qualification scale the expectation is for a decrease in the unskilled or low skilled workforce down from 29% to 19% by 2020. This trend was confirmed by the Confederation of British Industry (CBI) report, 'Ready to grow: education and skills report 2010', *"Businesses expect the make-up of the workforce to change rapidly in the next three to five years, with employer demand for low-level skills declining and 55% of firms reporting an increased need for more higher-skilled employees"*. [4] However, currently there are a worryingly high number of young people with few or no qualifications. The unskilled jobs of the industrial age that used to soak up the unqualified and offered advancement through 'learning on the job' and 'up-skilling' have largely gone. The following table indicates how over the last thirty years the numbers in work and in full-time education have dramatically altered in response to the decline of unskilled employment and the demand for higher qualifications.[5]

Category	Aged 18 1976 %	Aged 18 1988 %	Aged 18 2009 %
Employed	74	68	40
FT Education	17	25	45
Unemployed	9	7	16

Wolf Report, Review of Vocation education, March 2011.

There are unskilled jobs within the Knowledge Age economy but they are primarily within the service sector rather than factory employment and many have yet to adjust their expectations. The One North East Regional Development Agency in England reported in 2010 that, *"the majority of JSA claimants are seeking work in occupations typified by lower levels of qualification NVQ Level Two or below – for men elementary occupations process, plant and machine operatives and skilled trades….7 out of 10 men are looking for jobs as labourers, factory workers…"* [6] The industries that supplied such jobs have long gone and the future is bleak for school leavers without qualifications and who lack the skills or aptitude to enter the dominant service sector. The service sector even at an unqualified level requires well-presented young people with good literacy, numeracy, social and customer service skills. Careers advisers regularly have to advise young people to dress smartly, to cover visible tattoos, to remove face piercings, to tone down highly coloured or elaborate hairstyles and to moderate their language. What, in the past, may not have mattered on the factory floor does matter in an office or retail environment. The connection between qualifications and economic growth is highlighted by the following top five UK cities identified for either rising or falling economic growth by the Centre for Cities agency.

Top five UK cities for rising or falling economic growth 2011[7]

High prospects				Low prospects			
No	City	Employment Rate %	% High Quals*	No	City	Employment Rate %	% High Quals*
1	Aberdeen	78.5	41.4	1	Birkenhead	67.5	12.3
2	Reading	76.2	37.9	2	Newport	66.7	14.7
3	Bristol	74.2	33.2	3	Sunderland	64.9	13.2
4	Milton Keynes	72.5	33.7	4	Swansea	64.8	16.1
5	Leeds	70.4	30.9	5	Liverpool	62.7	19.5

*degree or equivalent qualifications

Source: Centre for Cities 2011.

The above table shows that the average UK employment rate is 70.4% and the average percentage of the workforce with high level qualifications is 29.9%. The cities with the highest prospects for growth all reflect well qualified workforces and vice versa. The same issue is evident in the United States with many 'dead' industrial towns struggling to raise achievement levels in order to attract new employers. This is a significant challenge because too many of our young people fail to settle at school and to make a success of their studies and many literally vote with their feet and play truant or drop out of school entirely. Poor retention and underachievement in any education system has multiple and overlapping causes but at its core are young people often from deprived backgrounds with limited or no home support who struggle to see a positive future and who struggle to see the benefits of engaging in education. The clear majority of young people around 85% stay on into Full-Time education but in 2013 the school leaving age will be raised to 17 and in 2015 to age 18 to bring England in line with most other European countries. Of these students 38% study Full-Time A-Levels, 7% Part-Time A-Levels, 21% other Level Three qualifications and a significant 34% Level Two or One qualifications. The latter group represents some 350,000 young people who will struggle to find future employment and the key learning target is to ensure the achievement of at least a Grade C in both GCSE English and Maths. Currently only 45% of the cohort gain a Grade C in both subjects by age 16 and by age 18 only a further 4% have studied and gained a Grade C in both English and Maths thereby raising the overall percentage to 49% but still less than half the cohort. Many will have studied vocational alternatives but the *Review of Vocational Education* report chaired by Professor Alison Wolf, March 2011 questioned the worth and value of such qualifications and has recommended that schools and colleges offer repeat GCSE courses and provide enhanced tuition to help as many as possible to achieve the GCSE standard. Wolf commented, '*No other developed country allows, let alone effectively encourages, its young people to neglect maths and their own language in this way*'. [8] The current Secretary of State, Michael Gove has accepted Wolf's recommendations and issued the following guidance in the Government White Paper, 'The importance of teaching' 2010, '*Students who are under 19 and do not have GCSE A*-C in English and/or Maths should be required, as part of their programme, to pursue a course which either leads directly to these qualifications, or which provide significant progress towards future GCSE entry and success*'.[9] The overall GCSE pass rates at age 16 are also low. In summer 2010 the national average in England for passing five GCSE examinations grades A*-C was 69.1% with a marginal increase to 69.8% in 2011. However, when English and Maths are included this percentage drops to 53.4%. This is a low outcome after eleven years of compulsory education but alarmingly the percentage drops to 28% for pupils from low income families. Poverty, with few exceptions, dictates

2002 one of President Bush's last acts as President was to sign into law the No Child Left Behind (NCLB) Act. The law attached higher federal funding to schools that hit achievement targets in a bid to spur schools and State Boards to stem the high number of school drop outs and arrest falling achievement rates. Despite this incentive few States have improved to the levels expected with most languishing around 20-30% in the proficiency targets for literacy and maths far below the headline drive for 100% achievement of the specified targets. In 2009 President Obama increased the incentive for schools to improve with the 'Race to the top' initiative which extended federal funding to the achievement of a wider range of improvement targets. In essence 'good' schools would gain higher funding to expand and poor schools would wither and ultimately close. The scale of the underperformance in U.S. schools was revealed in September 2010 by the release of the documentary film 'Waiting for Superman' by Davis Guggenheim. This documentary highlighted that high school 'drop outs' with no qualifications often matched, and in some districts, even exceeded the number of High School graduates to the extent that Guggenheim dismissed many of the schools as little more than, 'drop out factories'. On average a third of U.S. high school children do not graduate and when the data is crunched by ethnicity there is a significant 25-30% disparity between minority ethnic and majority White achievement rates but with poverty being the key determinant. The rising level of underachievement, in both the UK and the USA, (and other European states) threatens social cohesion because it can lead to a polarised society of the haves and the have-nots. Once too many feel that schools offer no advantage and with few jobs for the unskilled and unqualified whole districts and even whole towns can fall into dependency on welfare benefits and a non-work culture. This is a tragedy in particular for the individual(s) who often survive on very low incomes and for any dependants who may go on to repeat the cycle. It also has a significant cost for the wider community and wider economy. Guggenheim has highlighted that in the state of Pennsylvania 68% of the prison population were high school dropouts and that the cost to the taxpayer of an average prison sentence was greater than offering those in poverty a private education from birth. The same argument has been deployed in the UK in terms of the underachievement of children taken into care as against funding a place at a boarding school to give stability and continuity of personal development. Overall, there is an imperative here to question how we might improve our curriculum and pedagogy to meet the needs of those who are clearly telling us that the system doesn't work (for them). Andreas Schleicher who is the Head of the Indicators and Analysis Division of the Organisation of Economic Co-operation and Development (OECD) has stated: *If you were running a supermarket instead of a school and saw that 30 out of 100 customers each day left your shop without buying anything, you would think about changing your inventory. But that does not happen easily in schools because of deeply rooted, even if scientifically unsupported, beliefs that learning can only occur in a particular way.*[10]

Clearly the question arises that if some countries are so successful in engaging young people in learning and raising achievement levels what is it that they do?

The International Baccalaureate (ibo.org)

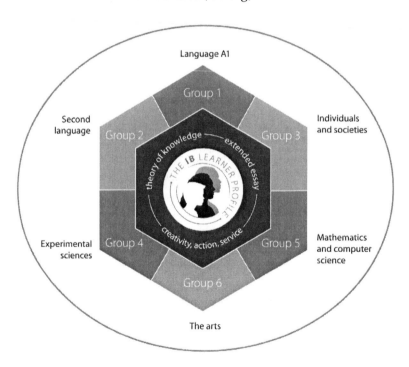

The curriculum model most often associated with a focus on skills, personal development, academic rigour and importantly breadth of knowledge is the International Baccalaureate (IB) which now offers three levels of programmes across Primary, Middle School and a Diploma for the 16-19 age-group. The Diploma introduces the challenge, *'Life in the 21st Century in an interconnected globalised world requires critical-thinking skills and a sense of international mindness...'* [11] The IB concept emerged out of United Nations Education, Scientific and Cultural Organisation (UNESCO) discussion papers as early as 1948 but it was not until 1968 that it was established as a non-profiting making charity with its headquarters in Geneva, Switzerland. Today the IB has won many converts and is offered by 3,285 schools across 141 countries and the Diploma is recognised by universities worldwide for admission. At the heart of the IB is the Learner Profile which identifies ten core skills, values and aptitudes which the IB programme aims to foster and develop. Regardless of the subjects selected the focus of the IB is the individual and stretching and challenging the students to be the best they can be within skills centred rather than knowledge centred programmes. The attraction of the IB, in particular, is a broad subject base which delivers a rich array of individual skills and knowledge across oral and written communication, calculation, data analysis, scientific method, investigation, research, analysis, evaluation, presentation, language, social awareness, cultural awareness and personal skills. This is a significant skills and knowledge platform for employment within the 21st century economy and supports a wide choice of career options.

The IB Learner profile

IB Learners will strive to be:	
Inquirers	**Open-minded**
They develop their natural curiosity. They acquire the skills necessary to conduct inquiry and research and show independence in learning. They actively enjoy learning and this love of learning will be sustained throughout their lives.	They understand and appreciate their own cultures and personal histories, and are open to the perspectives, values and traditions of other individuals and communities. They are accustomed to seeking and evaluating a range of points of view, and are willing to grow from the experience.
Knowledgeable	**Caring**
They explore concepts, ideas and issues that have local and global significance. In so doing, they acquire in-depth knowledge and develop understanding across a broad and balanced range of disciplines.	They show empathy, compassion and respect towards the needs and feelings of others. They have a personal commitment to service and act to make a positive difference to the lives of others and to the environment.

Thinkers	Risk-takers
They exercise initiative in applying thinking skills critically and creatively to recognise and approach complex problems and make reasoned, ethical decisions.	They approach unfamiliar situations and uncertainty with courage and forethought, and have the independence of spirit to explore new roles, ideas and strategies. They are brave and articulate in defending their beliefs
Communicators	**Balanced**
They understand and express ideas and information confidently and creatively in more than one language and in a variety of modes of communication. They work effectively and willingly in collaboration with others.	They understand the importance of intellectual, physical and emotional balance to achieve personal well-being for themselves and others.
Principled	**Reflective**
They act with integrity and honesty with a strong sense of fairness, justice and respect for the dignity of the individual, groups and communities. They take responsibility for their own actions and the consequences that accompany them.	They give thoughtful consideration to their own learning and experience. They are able to assess and understand their strengths and limitations in order to support their learning and personal development.

The development of a broad based and skills led curriculum is not exclusive to the IB but all too often too many students are permitted to specialise too early i.e. 14+ and enter a much narrower exam focussed dash. In contrast the IB Middle Years and Diploma programmes delay specialisation and provide and maintain a broad base of study. At Diploma level 16-19 learners must study six subjects chosen from six subject groups:

1. Home language and literature
2. Language acquisition (foreign language)
3. Individuals and Societies (Humanities and Social sciences)
4. Experimental sciences
5. Mathematics and computer science
6. Arts

It is compulsory to select a subject from the first five groups but the sixth subject may be from any group although the Arts are strongly encouraged. In addition all students must engage with three cross disciplinary themes:

- Extended Essay (personal selection of topic)
- Theory of Knowledge (reflecting on the philosophy, types and nature of knowledge)
- Creativity Action Service (enrichment activity beyond the classroom)

The Middle Years Programme (11-16 years) has a very similar structure but with the addition to the above Diploma subjects of Physical Education and Technology and a broader set of five cross curricular 'interaction' themes. The IB is widely admired for achieving a rigorous and highly effective marriage between skills and knowledge and striking a good balance between depth and breadth and in particular preparing young people for the demands of 21st century living and working.

Kunskapsskolan Education Programme (KED)

The Kunskapsskolan Education programme in Sweden has also attracted worldwide attention for its innovative approach to introducing a personalised learning experience, wholly focussed on the individual and supported by a rich online learning environment. Kunskapsskolan means knowledge school. The first were opened in Sweden in 2000 and today there are 33 schools in Sweden and in September 2010 three academies in London adopted the KED curriculum. The KED curriculum starts with the individual and captures their aims and ambitions as the basis of an agreed programme of study with the learner and his or her parent(s) or guardian(s). The programme is fulfilled via an individual timetable which directs attendance to specified lessons, lectures, coaching sessions and online 'portal' learning packages closely monitored by a personal learning coach on a weekly basis. The focus is not on membership of a class and whole class lessons but on the individual and their attachment to a range of relevant learning opportunities. A broad curriculum is endorsed with cross curricular themes and in England this is reflected in study across the full range of National Curriculum subjects. The approach is very flexible and builds the personal responsibility to learn and permits students to advance through the curriculum according to their ability level in each subject. The following diagram illustrates the KED curriculum model with the student placed firmly at the centre.

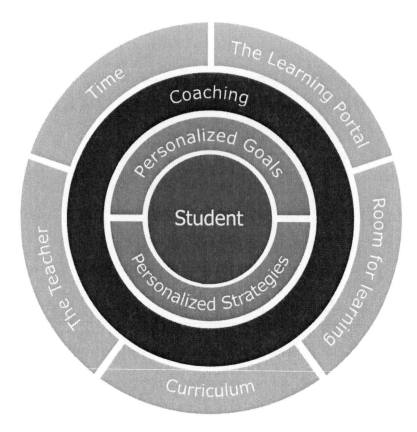

Applying the IB model

The provision of a holistic 'person centred' learning experience is not exclusive to the IB or the Kunskapsskolan schools but thrives in many schools and colleges in different countries and in many different forms. However, the opposite is equally true and there are perhaps more pupils and students who study very narrow programmes. In addition the development of Functional Skills in terms of Communication, Number and IT and wider independent research skills are often treated, and perceived by students, as 'bolt-on' extras rather than 'core' or integral to all subjects and central to their future employability and personal development. These issues have been much debated and reported over the past 20 years across the European Union, United States, Australia and England and a general curriculum consensus has emerged:

• Learning should be holistic and conceptual rather than purely functional,

- A broad knowledge is preferable to a narrow knowledge,
- Specialisation should occur Post 16 at the earliest,
- Academic and vocational subjects should be accorded equal status,
- Core skills including Communication, Number and IT should be fully integrated,
- Extended projects should provide stretch and challenge,
- An awareness of wider cultures and proficiency in foreign languages should be developed,
- All should be encouraged to be active citizens and to promote equality,
- All should gain opportunities for creativity and making a personal contribution.

Clearly the adoption of the IB or Kunskapsskolan model would address all or most of those curriculum goals but most countries prefer to develop 'home-grown' programmes. The issue is public recognition and 'comfort' with established national qualifications and most politicians with an eye on public opinion choose to try and incorporate existing qualifications within an IB style framework. There have been varying degrees of success with even some individual schools and colleges independently re-organising and re-branding their curriculum as a Baccalaureate. However, the speed of technological change and the need for a more highly skilled future workforce is driving a renewed re-think of the curriculum. One key driver is rising awareness that in comparison to other countries and particularly the Pacific Rim nations the UK and the United States are underperforming in terms of higher level skills across the core subjects of Reading (literacy), Maths and Science. Other nations are forging ahead while we are falling behind the curve as evidenced by the Pisa international comparative rankings.

Pisa top ten national rankings 2009

The Organisation for Economic Co-operation and Development (OECD) regularly monitors and conducts educational performance surveys against agreed international benchmarks. A key benchmark for education is Pisa i.e. Programme for International School Assessment (PISA) which compares and reports standards and achievements across the world's leading economies every three years.

The most recent Pisa report for 2009, but published 2010, may be accessed on the OECD website www.oecd.org/education. The report identifies achievement rates in standardised tests for Reading, Maths and Science taken by 15 year old pupils in 65 participating countries. The table below lists the rank order of the top ten performing nations.[12]

Reading (literacy)	Maths	Science
Shanghai -China	Shanghai-China	Shanghai-China
South Korea	Singapore	Finland
Finland	Hong Kong-China	Hong Kong-China
Hong Kong-China	South Korea	Singapore
Singapore	Chinese-Taipei	Japan
Canada	Finland	South Korea
New Zealand	Liechtenstein	New Zealand
Japan	Switzerland	Canada
Australia	Japan	Estonia
Netherlands	Canada	Australia

Shanghai is ranked Number One in each category in confirmation of China's rapid economic rise and high investment in education. The test margins were also significant with 25% of children from Shanghai demonstrating advanced mathematical abilities against an OECD average of only 3%. Shanghai and several other Chinese provinces have populations larger than many of the countries in the survey creating a significant pool of highly qualified graduates. Across the three categories only five countries earned a place within each top ten ranking:

- China
- Singapore
- South Korea
- Japan
- Canada

The above five countries enjoy high participation rates and high achievement rates. Most European countries, including the United Kingdom, are lower down the rank orders around the OECD average.

In terms of Literacy (reading) the UK is ranked in 25th place and the USA in 17th place, lower for Maths at 28th and 30th places respectively but with better performances for Science, hovering above the OECD average, with 16th and 23rd places respectively. Those results represent a significant drop for the United Kingdom. In 2000 the UK enjoyed a Pisa world ranking of 8th for literacy, 7th for Mathematics and 4th for Science although this was within a smaller pool of participating nations. The Pisa rankings highlight the rapid rise of the Pacific Rim states as significant investments in education succeed in raising achievement levels. South Korea is a potent example of a nation that has become a technological giant within the last thirty years through significant investment in education. The one edge still largely retained by the western world is creativity and it will be important to nurture and grow this edge in terms of new products, new technology and new services. In 2011 the European Union announced a plan to invest £6bn in the creation of 'innovation parks' to encourage and create bonds between hi-tech industries and university research centres. The future may be made in China but hopefully designed in the Europe? However, our creative edge is also under threat because China is heavily investing in scientific and industrial research and filing a significantly high number of patents. Our window of opportunity to build a more highly qualified, creative and innovative workforce is fast shrinking.

U.S. Partnership 21

China's first World Expo to showcase Chinese industry was held in 1999 and as reported in Chapter One was opened under the banner, *'Marching into the 21st Century'*. It was a stimuli to reform and in 2001 the United States launched the Partnership 21 initiative (www.p21.org) to re-think the U.S. curriculum in terms of 21st Century readiness across the knowledge and skills required for new industries and the expanding service sector. P21 is supported by the U.S. Department of Education and involves a consortium of key educators, visionaries, industrialists and teachers to review and guide curriculum reform. In a similar vision to the IB the focus is the individual in terms of personal skills development integrated across a core of broad academic knowledge, ' *Those who can think critically and communicate effectively must build on a base of core academic subject knowledge. Within the context of core knowledge instruction, students must also learn the essential skills for success in today's world, such as critical thinking, problem solving, communication and collaboration....students are more engaged in the learning process and graduate better prepared to thrive in today's global economy'*[13] Partnership 21 has identified a *Framework for 21st Century Learning* as illustrated below. The rainbow arch highlights the key recommended curriculum content in terms of skills and knowledge and the underpinning ripples the support systems.

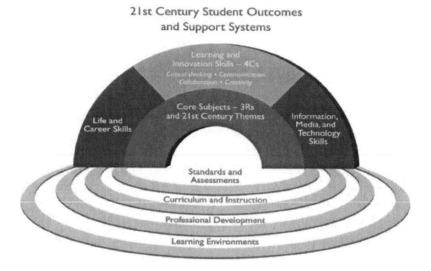

At the top of the rainbow arch are the 4Cs in terms of significant personal skills development as the core of classroom practice i.e. Critical thinking, Communication, Collaboration and Problem Solving and Creativity. Below are the Core Subjects referred as the 3Rs as shorthand for the traditional core subjects of English, Maths, Science, Humanities and Foreign Languages. In addition all staff are expected to develop and promote, awareness and understanding across five cross curriculum 21st Century themes:

- Global awareness,
- Financial, economic, business and entrepreneurial literacy,
- Civic literacy,
- Health literacy,
- Environmental literacy.

This curriculum model adopts a similar approach to the IB in terms of the importance of maintaining a broad subject base coupled with a firm development focus on the individual and coaching and drawing out their personal and employability skills. The supporting arches of the rainbow highlight the importance of careers guidance to help each individual to develop personal career goals and Information Technology and Media Skills to support the ability to learn and for future social and employment interactions. Finally the rainbow model identifies as its foundation five support systems to underpin the implementation of the new curriculum

1. 21st Century standards – *commitment to and actions to embed the new standards*
2. Assessment of 21st Century Skills – *ensuring effective formative and summative assessment techniques and the development of learner portfolios to showcase skills*
3. 21st Century curriculum and instruction – *competency led outcomes, innovation in classroom practice and use of technology and community involvement*
4. 21st Century Professional development – guiding and supporting teachers to develop and apply 21st century skills
5. 21st Century learning environments – *building the infrastructure to support 21st century learning*

The rainbow model presents a neat, at-a-glance, summary of the key elements of a 21st century curriculum and how the different elements of the curriculum might interlock to create a holistic programme of personal, career, academic and skills development. Its strength is the establishment of a shared vision and unity of purpose between employers, policy makers and teachers to underpin and drive forward change. The urgency of change to meet international competition was emphasised by the US Government report, *'New Commission on the skills of the American workforce'* published in 2006 which identified the importance of creativity, in particular, to future growth. Similar elements exist within the British educational system if we consider the National Curriculum, Personal, Social Education ,Health and Economic education (PSHE), Every Child Matters, Standard Assessment Tests, Thinking and Learning Skills, 14-19 Diplomas, Functional skills etc. However, as is the case with constitutions the U.S. model is written whereas the UK model is unwritten and no one has yet joined-up all the elements.

A British Baccalaureate

The UK has been flirting with the introduction of IB style programmes since the 1990s but whereas both Wales and Scotland have successfully introduced IB style frameworks progress in England has foundered on the reluctance to alter the A-Level 'gold standard'. In 1988 the Higginson Committee report proposed five 'lean' A-Levels in place of the standard programme of three A-Levels to introduce a broader curriculum with a core programme of personal and social skills. The report chaired by Sir Gordon Higginson was rejected for straying beyond its brief from review into reform and the suggestions were shelved. However, the debate was raised and in 1990 David Miliband, now a senior member of the Labour Party, was one of six accredited authors of a pamphlet entitled, 'A British Baccalaureate: overcoming divisions between education and training'. The pamphlet, published by the Institute for Public Policy Research, focussed on the merits of the IB to bridge the academic / vocational divide and to broaden opportunity. The narrow study of three subjects at A-Level was widely regarded not as an 'education' but merely a ticket to Higher Education and something that served the needs of only a third of the 14-19 age-group. In addition, out of those who entered A-Level approximately 70% passed, 17% failed and 13% dropped out early amounting to around 80,000 students per year who either failed to complete or pass A-Level. This was a significant pool of disadvantaged young people and fuelled further pressure for reform but it was nearly a decade later before there was sufficient support for change. In 1996 a curriculum review by Sir Ron Dearing deepened Higginson's proposal and recommended the division of the two year A-Level programme into modular AS and A2 qualifications so that most students would gain at least an interim AS award. Dearing envisaged students studying up to five AS subjects in their first year with three subjects carried forward into A2 along with the study of Key Skills in Communication, Numeracy and IT. The new structure was accepted but in practice few students studied five AS subjects and most selected complementary rather than contrasting subjects which increased rather than decreased specialisation. Key Skills were also reduced to a bolt-on extra rather than embedded across all subjects and were not particularly valued by most students. Dearing's proposals for a complete reform of the whole 14-19 curriculum within an overarching diploma framework found no favour. However, any discussion of the broadening of the school curriculum should embrace and look to extend the success of 14-16 school-college vocational programmes. Many young people would benefit from a 14+ vocational programme but a vocational programme that is regarded as a significant parallel stream to the academic GCSE and A-Level pathway. Britain has a very poor record of celebrating vocational success evidenced by the annual media and political jamboree that accompanies the release of A-Level results every August compared to the next to no media coverage of the annual Vocational Qualifications (VQ) day in July. Most of the public are probably unaware that there is an annual VQ day and even the World Skills Championships, held in London in October 2011, with an array of highly impressive vocational skills on display, scarcely gained a mention in the media. The vocational pathway is all too often devalued and stronger 14-16 school / college partnerships should be forged. The curriculum reform debate was renewed in 2004 with the publication of the *'Working Group on 14-19 reform'* otherwise known as the Tomlinson Report after Chairman, Mike Tomlinson. Eighteen months of deliberation resulted in a far-reaching proposal to fully rebrand all 14-19 qualifications within a Diploma framework including a programme of fully integrated common core skills and an extended project to stretch and challenge the most able. Like the IB model Tomlinson placed personal skills development at the heart of the framework

'We propose that the core, common to all programmes and diplomas, should comprise:

- *functional mathematics;*
- *functional literacy and communication;*
- *functional ICT;*
- *an extended project;*
- *common knowledge, skills and attributes (CKSA);*
- *personal review, planning and guidance; and*
- *an entitlement to wider activities'.*[14]

The CKSA element related to wider social awareness with a raft of personal development proposals across three major themes and completion was a compulsory aspect of the diploma:

- *The reflective and effective individual learner,*
- *The social learner and*
- *The learner in society and the wider world*

'The core would ensure that young people acquire the functional mathematics, functional literacy and communication, functional ICT and common knowledge, skills and attributes (CKSA) they require to succeed and progress in learning, HE, employment and adult life. No young person would be able to achieve a diploma without having acquired them'. [15]

The above skills focus addressed the challenge of living and working in the 21st Century and coupled with the curriculum proposals represented very much the creation of a broad based British Baccalaureate. However, the timing was unfortunate because with elections in the offing the report was shelved as a hot potato and thereafter only found expression as the basis of the new 14-19 vocational Diploma programmes introduced in 2005. Currently there is no political appetite to extend the Diploma, as originally planned, into academic subjects and despite twenty years of debate around the benefits of an IB style curriculum and parity of esteem between A-Level and vocational programmes progress remains elusive. The irony of course is that the 'Gold Standard' was abandoned in 1931 for a broader measure of national wealth. There was a further glimmer of change 2007-08 but a modest proposal for every Local Authority in England to offer the IB, in at least one centre, as an alternative to the narrow A-Level curriculum also withered away.

Cambridge Pre-U

The demand for a broader based qualification has led to rising interest in the new Cambridge International Examinations (CIE) board Pre-University or Pre-U qualification introduced in 2008. The Pre-U endorses the principles of a broad curriculum and the integration of personal learning and thinking skills via a core of three principal subjects, an independent research report and a global perspectives study.

The qualification is aimed at university progression but it does reflect the context of a rapidly changing 21st century economy, *"The Cambridge Pre-U Diploma is rooted in subject specialisation, but through its core components, it develops the skills necessary to deal with the complex,*

Independent research report		
Principal subject	**Principal subject**	**Principal subject**
Global perspectives study		

connected and rapidly changing world in which students live, study and work". [16] The development of skills to be a successful learner and for future employment are regarded as integral plus the development of a wider international outlook in a reflection of more integrated and global economy, *"helping learners to acquire specific skills of problem solving, critical thinking, creativity, team-working, independent learning and effective communication".* [17] The Pre-U offers a promising home-grown alternative to the narrow A-Level curriculum. The successful development of the Pre-U has perhaps promoted recent proposals from the Office for Qualifications (Ofqual) in England for the injection of an extended project into the A-Level curriculum to help develop the research and independent learning skills vital for university success.

An English Baccalaureate

The broad v narrow education debate was re-ignited in 2010 by concern over the low number of young people maintaining a study of STEM related subjects i.e. Science, Technology, Engineering and Mathematics 14-19. STEM subjects are in high demand by rising hi-tech industries but in contrast to most advanced economies young people in England can abandon whole disciplines at age 14 and have no further exposure to Science, Maths, Foreign Languages or Humanities. The narrow A-Level curriculum is the product of the narrow 14-16 GCSE curriculum. The greatest casualties are Science and Maths and consequently at degree level in the UK, on average, only 8% of students study Engineering, Manufacturing or Construction compared to 26% opting for Humanities, Arts or

Education. The former is a small pool and whereas it may be beneficial for the individuals in terms of higher than average employment and salary prospects for the wider economy it places a question-mark over the UK capacity to grow and expand hi-tech industries. The Wolf report 2011 criticised narrow curriculum options for providing no progression, *"the UK is effectively unique in not requiring continual mathematics and own-language study for all young people engaged in 16-19 and pre-tertiary education…Instead they have been steered into courses (or simply into tests) of 'Key Skills', which are simple and, in progression terms valueless".*[18] Wolf has recommended the maintenance of a broad GCSE curriculum to age 16 for 80% of the school timetable with vocational and other optional choices limited to 20% of the timetable or when expressed as days a 4+1 model.

A core GCSE programme

The current Secretary of State for Education, Michael Gove, has accepted Wolf's conclusions and recommended in the Government White Paper, 'The Importance of Teaching' 2010 the adoption of an 'English Baccalaureate' i.e. a common core subject base for all young people to age 16, *'In most European countries school students are expected to pursue a broad and rounded range of academic subjects until the age of 16. …So we will introduce a new award – the English Baccalaureate – for any student who secures good GCSE or iGCSE passes in English, mathematics, the sciences, a modern or ancient foreign language and a humanity such as history or geography'.* [19]

A common core GCSE programme

The above recommended programme is a loose arrangement of existing GCSE subjects around a core of Personal, Social and Health Education (PSHE) as the broadening factor. Only a minority (23%) of the 2011 GCSE cohort studied such a broad curriculum and the national average pass rate for passing all six Ebac subjects at Grades A*-C was only 16.5 % in 2011 which is a slight rise from 15.6% in 2010. These are alarming statistics for our future capability to expand hi-tech industries and a major challenge for some deprived districts in England where the average Ebac pass rate drops as low as 3%. The English Baccalaureate is not curriculum reform but rather curriculum specification and without major changes to the pedagogy the

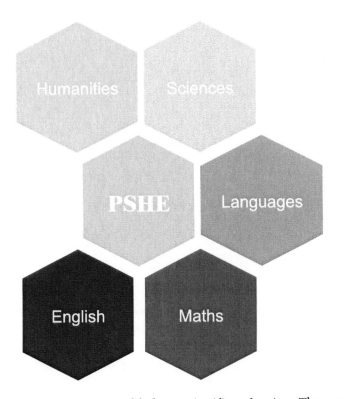

achievement rates are unlikely to significantly rise. Those who struggle today will still struggle tomorrow without a review of existing pedagogical practice and how to fully engage more young people in learning. Therefore the key consideration is not so much *what* we teach but *how* we teach and increasingly the answer is the Virtual Learning Environment (VLE) both to extend subject knowledge and to build the skills required for 21st century employment.

5 21st century skills

"NOW, what I want is, Facts. Teach these boys and girls nothing but Facts. Facts alone are wanted in life. Plant nothing else, and root out everything else. You can only form the minds of reasoning animals upon Facts: nothing else will ever be of any service to them. This is the principle on which I bring up my own children, and this is the principle on which I bring up these children. Stick to Facts, sir!" [1]

Thomas Gradgrind speaking to a schoolmaster in Hard Times by
Charles Dickens 1853

Dicken's *Hard Times* was a critique of the harsh industrial conditions prevalent in Nineteenth Century England and the words of his character Gradgrind reflected a predominant attitude to education i.e. highly utilitarian with nothing creative or in Gradgrind's words 'fancy'. However, advances in our society arise from curiosity, questions, hypotheses or 'flights of fancy' in general rather than mere repetition. To repeat or to copy is to standstill. Many inventions and discoveries are a result of curiosity and accidental discovery including Saccharin, Plastics, Teflon, Penicillin, Post-it Notes, Coca Cola and most recently Microscopic Sensors popularly known as 'Smart Dust'. When the zipper began to replace buttons in 1914 it was thought to be the last possible innovation in clothes fastening until the appearance of Velcro in 1970s. Our most successful companies do not standstill but embrace change and innovation. In 1993 it seemed that vacuum cleaner technology could not evolve any further until Sir James Dyson invented the bag-less cyclone vacuum cleaner. Within five years the Dyson dominated world sales of vacuum cleaners and today it would be more accurate to talk of dysoning the carpet rather than hoovering it. Industry thrives on creativity and innovation and for most companies this translates into a core of effective team working skills, confident communication, accurate numeracy and comfortable rather than emerging IT skills. As Chapter One has documented manufacturing employment has migrated East and the 21st century economy will be built on hi- tech industries supported by world class business, finance and banking services and the 'people facing' service sector. Our young people are entering a global market place and to thrive and enjoy rewarding careers they need to be as James Dyson has commented 'polymaths' i.e. highly skilled, creative and versatile individuals alert to cultural differences and proactive in their approach to winning and sustaining customer satisfaction. Consequently merely teaching young people a set of facts to repeat in an examination will not assist them nor future economic growth. The facts are essential – it is a false dichotomy to offer facts or skills we can have both. The facts lead but skills must follow. Consequently schools and colleges need to focus on 'process' to ensure that young people have regular opportunities to practise and hone the interpersonal and intrapersonal skills required for employment within a fast changing, global, 21st century economy. The importance of skills was confirmed by the Confederation of British Industry (CBI) survey of employers 2011 in response to the question, *'What are the most important factors considered when employing graduates?'* [2]

Figure 1

Recruitment consideration	% agreement
Employability skills	82
Degree subject	68
Relevant work experience	62
Degree result	50
University attended	8
Foreign language capability	4

The majority of employers surveyed ranked employability skills as more significant than degree subject and despite the primacy often accorded to a Russell Group degree the university attended is far down the table. The CBI first highlighted the importance of employability skills over degree subject in 2008. However, this focus on the individual and encouraging their personal abilities and skills is not new. Consider the following extract from the Elementary School Code for England first published in 1904 *"the aim of the School is to train the children carefully in the habits of observation and clear reasoning so that they may gain an intelligent acquaintance with some of the facts and laws of nature; to arouse in them a living interest in the ideas and achievements of mankind, and to bring to them some familiarity with the literature and history of their own country; to give them some power over language as an instrument of though and expression, and, while making them conscious of the limitations of their knowledge, to develop in them such a taste for good reading and thoughtful study as will enable them to increase that knowledge in after years by their own efforts... Afford them every opportunity for the healthy development of their bodies not only by training them in appropriate physical exercises and encouraging them in organised games by instructing them in the working of some of the simpler laws of health...It will be an important though subsidiary object of the School to discover individual children who show promise of exceptional capacity and to develop their special gifts... The School should implant in the children habits of industry, self control and courageous perseverance in the face of difficulties... To strive their utmost after purity and truth...To foster a strong sense of duty and instil in them that consideration and respect for others which must be the foundations of unselfishness and the true basis of good manners".* [3]

Over 100 years later it would be hard to disagree with those aspirations and they perhaps express a more holistic view of education than the 'Tina Turner' style mission statements adopted by some colleges and schools. The first public schools in England (i.e state funded schools as distinct from private fee-paying schools open to the public) were introduced by the *Elementary Education Act* in 1870 for children aged 5-10. Then, as now, the stimulus was concern that Britain was falling behind in industrial development in comparison to fast-developing nations like Prussia (nucleus of modern Germany) and that a more literate and numerate workforce was crucial to Britain's future prosperity. Consequently the first schools focussed on raising standards in the 3Rs reading, writing and arithmetic. There were six levels of attainment and the sixth and highest level targets were specified as follows in Figure Two:

1870 3Rs targets

Figure 2

Reading	to read with fluency and expression
Writing	A short theme or letter or an easy paraphrase
Arithmetic	Proportion and fractions: vulgar and decimal

for more serious researchers how to operate the microfiche young people in the 21st Century need to be highly proficient in digital research and search skills to sift the digital wheat from the digital chaff. All need to know the limitations and effectiveness of different search engines and how to use advanced search techniques to limit and refine hits e.g. using a .gov search will just return information from official government departments. Our students and future employees must also be able to discriminate and evaluate the usefulness, source and credibility of digital information and how to organise, reference, store and protect it. The **Communication Dimension** is equally important in terms of the ability to analyse and evaluate information and to present findings in the most appropriate form including confidence in using statistics and number. It is common for many teachers to complain about a 'cut and paste' culture among the rising i-generations but how far are the skills of effective research and communication modelled, taught and developed? In terms of presentation the digital age offers an array of possibilities across video, podcasts, developing a wiki, creating a poster, using social networking sites, creating a photo slideshow, adding to a website, designing a website, writing a blog, writing a formal report, publishing an e-book or to the more familiar oral presentation supported by Powerpoint or perhaps Prezi. Few would present data as a pie chart when tree and cloud tags now dominate our corporate publications. Everyone loves wordle.net. Comfort and familiarity with relevant industry standard software is essential e.g. Microsoft Office or within the creative industries Apple and perhaps relevant specialist applications like Sage for accountancy etc. Microsoft Office unfolds into Word, Powerpoint, Excel, Access, and Publisher and as far as possible our students should learn to navigate and apply these programs with ease. Although we teach a digital generation their digital skills can exist within a narrow field i.e. they may leave you standing when navigating itunes but be uncertain how to manipulate a spreadsheet. Students and employees also need to appreciate the difference between a mashup and plagiarism i.e. one is creativity and the other is copying and how to reference as appropriate. Communication tasks might also involve paired or team-working and this is a significant competency not only to be able to work well with other people but to a deadline. **The Ethics and Social Impact** dimension reflects the scale of personal interactions as developments in mobile computing, hot desking, home working, 24 hour access, online shopping, online communication, multicultural society, global trade etc significantly alters our patterns of living and working and raises issues related to sustainability, exploitation and fair trade. In this fast-changing environment our personal skills are significant to build and sustain productive and culturally sensitive relationships. Individuals must also be alert to the risks of social networking and safeguarding their personal information and allied to this responsibility in their personal use of digital information networks. Bullying by text is already a significant problem in our schools and many at work regret a Friday night update or photograph on Facebook or an ill-judged email. Employers are increasingly alert to the online world and many complete Facebook, You Tube and Google searches as part of background checks on potential employees. The three OECD dimensions collectively identify *digital competency* as the defining 21st Century skill and one that should be reflected across all aspects of school and/or college life. At the very least it is time to dust off the standard study skills questionnaire used at induction and to recast as a digital competency questionnaire to inform digital skills development.

OECD digital competencies survey

The Organisation for Economic Co-Operation and Development (OECD) digital competencies survey distinguished between basic internet tasks and high level ICT tasks to gauge the competence levels of a representative sample of students across member states. The percentages, as displayed in Figure Three overleaf, reveal the extent of student confidence across a range of digital skills.

As might be expected much more confidence is expressed in relation to the internet tasks rather than ICT tasks. Clearly our students are less familiar with the high level ICT tasks but 'with help' most are confident they could manage. There is no, 'no' column, something Vygotsky would approve of, (see Chapter Nine) because of the positive assumption that with appropriate help all can improve and develop their skills. The integration of opportunities to practice and develop digital competencies should be a standard feature of our lesson and course planning. In 2010 the OECD recommended, *'Governments should make an effort to identify and conceptualise the required set of skills and competencies so as to incorporate them into the*

Figure 3 OECD Digital competencies survey[5]

Internet task	% Yes	% Yes with help
Search the internet for information	91	5
Download files or programs from the internet	75	16
Attach a file to an email message	72	16
Download music from the internet	75	15
Write an send email	83	10
Chat on-line	82	9
High level ICT tasks	**% Yes**	**% Yes with help**
Use software to find or get rid of viruses	44	29
Create a database i.e. using Microsoft Access	25	31
Edit digital photographs or other graphic images	58	26
Use a spreadsheet to plot a graph	48	31
Create a presentation i.e. using Microsoft Powerpoint	58	25
Creating a multimedia presentation i.e with sound, pictures and video.	44	35
Construct a web page	31	38
Use a wordprocessor e.g. to write an essay	82	11

educational standards that every student should be able to meet by the end of compulsory schooling'. [6] The digital skills questionnaire, presented in Appendix A, is suggested as a way to gauge the level of student skills across different aspects of ICT skills and internet access. The questionnaire might also be a useful way to raise discussion and awareness of staff internet and ICT skills given the OECD comment, *'there are clear indications that the pace of technology adoption is slower than expected or, in other words, that the pace of technology adoption by teachers is slower than in other sectors or even at home'.* [7] In other words the integration and regular use of ICT in our classrooms is at a lower level than most areas of employment and even within most students' homes. It is not unusual to see OHPs and video machines still in classrooms even when an Interactive White Board is mounted on the wall and to discover few resources to support and extend learning on Virtual Learning Environments (VLE). Consequently the key issue for our schools and colleges, as evidenced by the OECD, is no longer physical access to computers and the internet but the application of the technology by teachers to support teaching and learning, *'The main factor explaining frequency of use is to be found in the professional thinking and motivation of teachers…Clearly the installed base of equipment and connectivity infrastructure in schools remains underutilised'.*[8] Essentially the limited use of technology in our classrooms is more of a software than a hardware issue i.e. the computers and Interactive White Boards exist but the issue is one of the skills and confidence levels of teachers. However, there are other factors at work which slow the adoption and application of ICT by teachers:

- Insufficient 'hands on' time to build confidence,
- A bewildering array of resources to choose from,
- A lack of exemplar applications to demonstrate added value,
- Insufficient involvement of teachers in the design and functions of Virtual Learning Environments (VLEs),
- The barrier of technical language.

Busy teachers need easy access to ICT training and this is best addressed by a buddy system of pairing staff, peer observations, short workshops, help files and You Tube style self-access videos to explain key functions and applications. Each curriculum area also needs an ICT Champion so that 'how to…' guidance is only a few desks away. Finally, all departments or programme areas should discuss and set an IT development strategy with measurable targets rather than leaving IT developments to a few enthusiasts. Without actions of this type to support and develop staff skills the adoption and use of ICT will remain slow and the preserve of enthusiasts rather than the habit of all staff. However, teachers must also help themselves and those who boast of their lack of ICT skills must realise that this is no longer tenable. Lifelong Learning applies to teachers just as much as the students we seek to inspire.

Vision 2020 report

In 2006 the Vision 2020 review group, chaired by the past Chief Inspector of Ofsted (Office for standards in Education), Christine Gilbert, attempted to define more closely the changing employment landscape and the significant generic skills for future employment. Vision 2020 recommended movement to a personalised learning curriculum and the development of personal learning skills, *'Schools have a central role in helping pupils to develop the skills and attitudes for learning, on which they can draw throughout their lives… these are as much* the hard currency of learning as, say, knowledge of subject content'.[9] Vision 2020 challenged schools to plan for the employment market of 2020:

- *an ethnically and socially diverse society in which the gaps in achievement and prospects for people from different social and ethnic backgrounds will not be allowed to persist,*
- *far greater access to, and reliance on technology as a means of conducting daily interactions and transactions,*
- *a knowledge-based economy where it will be possible to compete with developing and global markets only by offering products and services of high quality, matched closely to customers' needs,*
- *demanding employers, who are clear about the skills their businesses need and value*
- *complex pathways through education and training, requiring young people to make choices and reach decisions,*
- *a sharper focus on sustainability, the role of individuals within their communities, and their impact on the environment.*

In addition the Vision 2020 report specified the importance of the following significant generic skills:

- *being able to communicate orally at a high level,*
- *reliability, punctuality and perseverance,*
- *knowing how to work with others in a team,*
- *knowing how to evaluate information critically,*
- *taking responsibility for, and being able to manage, one's own learning and developing the habits of effective learning,*
- *knowing how to work independently without close supervision,*
- *being confident and able to investigate problems and find solutions,*
- *being resilient in the face of difficulties,*
- *being creative, inventive, enterprising and entrepreneurial.*[10]

Few would disagree with the importance of this checklist but too few lessons offer regular opportunities for research, investigation, discussion, evaluation and creative presentation to build and develop skills of this type. Vision 2020 reported in 2006, *"However, many pupils report that their experience of school is still marked by long periods of time listening to teachers or copying from the board or a book".*[11] The most recent Ofsted Chief Inspector's Report published November 2011 reported that 42% of the lessons in our secondary sector are no better than satisfactory and noted, *"Activities tend to be insufficiently challenging, are not well matched to the needs of the pupils and are often based on procedural and descriptive work. The level of challenge for more able pupils is a particular issue. Lessons and learning are not well-paced, with time lost on unproductive activities such as copying out the objectives for the lesson , completing exercises without sufficient reason or simply spending too long on one activity"*. [12] Therefore it is important for schools and colleges to raise the importance of planning lessons that are more involving and build skills as well as knowledge because we can have both. Skills and knowledge are not mutually exclusive.

Assessment and Teaching of 21st Century Skills

The issue of a skills driven curriculum and how best to define and assess generic skills is at the heart of the Assessment and Teaching of 21st Century Skills project (www.atc21s.org). The 21st Century Skills project is an international consortium of educationalists providing leadership and research to build a consensus of the most significant skills for the 21st Century economy. The leading member nations are:

Australia,
Finland,
Portugal,
Singapore,
United Kingdom and
United States of America.

The project was launched 13th January 2009 and is based in Melbourne University, Australia and supported by Cisco, Intel and Microsoft. The project website provides the following mission statement:[13]

"Today's curricula does not fully prepare students to live and work in an information-age society. As a result, employers today are often challenged with entry-level workers who lack the practical skills it takes to create, build and help sustain an information-rich business.

Although reading, writing, mathematics and science are cornerstones of today's education, curricula must go further to include skills such as collaboration and digital literacy that will prepare students for 21st-century employment. Establishing new forms of assessment can begin a fundamental change in how we approach education worldwide".

The project has published five 'white papers' to promote discussion and as a basis for on-going research and these may be downloaded from the project website. The first White Paper entitled, *'What are 21st Century skills'?* introduces the KSAVE framework as a focus for skills development and assessment. Ten significant skills for future living and working are specified across four major themes as follows

The KSAVE Framework[14]

Ways of Thinking
1. Creativity and innovation
2. Critical thinking, problem solving, decision making
3. Learning to learn, Metacognition

Ways of Working
4. Communication
5. Collaboration (teamwork)

Tools for Working
6. Information literacy
7. ICT literacy

Living in the World
8. Citizenship – local and global
9. Life and career
10. Personal & social responsibility – including cultural awareness and competence

The initials KSAVE refer to Knowledge, Skills, Attitudes, Values and Ethics. Two of the above skills, *'Collaborative problem solving'* and *'ICT Literacy – learning in digital networks'* are identified as important unifying skills across all four themes. The significance of KSAVE is the establishment of an internationally agreed benchmark and definition of 21st Century Skills. Ultimately the major project goal is to release 'rights free' software to aid the development and assessment of 21st century skills. The skills identified by KSAVE reflect the skills identified as important by the Vision 2020 and the Confederation of British Industry (CBI). The omission of numeracy or any form of mathematical skills is surprising given the core importance of skills related to number and statistical analysis across most areas of employment. However this may be corrected in the final publication.

CBI Employability skills 2011

The Confederation of British Industry (CBI) represents the views of many British employers nationally and since 2008 they have engaged in surveying their members' opinions on employability skills. The CBI has specified the importance of the following seven employability skills and invited schools and colleges to consider their integration into teaching and learning:

Self-management – readiness to accept responsibility, flexibility, time management, readiness to improve own performance

Teamworking – respecting others, co-operating, negotiating/persuading, contributing to discussions

Business and customer awareness – basic understanding of the key drivers for business success and the need to provide customer satisfaction

Problem solving – analysing facts and circumstances and applying creative thinking to develop appropriate solutions

Communication and literacy – application of literacy, ability to produce clear, structured
written work and oral literacy, including listening and questioning

Application of numeracy – manipulation of numbers, general mathematical awareness
and its application in practical contexts

Application of information technology – basic IT skills, including familiarity with word processing, spreadsheets, file management and use of internet search engines

Since 2008 the CBI has conducted an annual survey of employers' satisfaction rates with the employability skills of school leavers and graduates. Their most recent report, published in May 2011, was entitled, *'Building for Growth: education and skills survey'* and provided an update to the 2010 report *'Ready to grow: education and skills survey'*. Employers in both surveys expressed their opinions across a range of employability skills as follows.

CBI Employer satisfaction with employability skills survey 2011[6]

Figure 4

Skills aspect	Very Satisfied%		Satisfied %		Not Satisfied%	
School Leaver (SL) and Graduate (Grad)	SL	Grad	SL	Grad	SL	Grad
Use of IT	19	33	69	62	12	5
Basic numeracy	5	20	59	70	35	9
Basic literacy / use of English	6	18	53	65	42	17
Teamwork	5	9	63	71	32	20
Positive attitude to work	7	17	58	68	35	15
Knowledge about job / career	4	11	51	64	45	24
Problem solving	3	11	54	70	43	19
Relevant work experience	2	5	42	54	56	42
International cultural awareness	1	6	37	50	61	43
Self-management	1	8	44	68	55	25
Business and customer awareness	2	5	29	50	69	44
Foreign language skills	1	4	23	36	76	60

The percentages have been rounded-up to the nearest whole number

The 2011 report shows a slight rise in employer satisfaction rates from 2010 but largely reflects a standstill. The 'use of IT' gains the highest satisfaction ratings and no doubt reflects the digital skills of the rising i-generations but many still lack competences in work applied IT i.e. comfortable across Microsoft Office. Around a third of employers remain dissatisfied with school-leavers' command of numeracy and although graduates perform much better the 42% and 14% dissatisfaction rates , respectively, for use of English raise concern. Beyond the core Functional Skills of IT, English and Numeracy the satisfaction levels drop off quite rapidly across the wider aspects of employability skills. Skills in Foreign languages drop to the lowest levels of employer satisfaction and this perhaps reflects that most

92

young people drop foreign languages at age 14. The top five 'in demand' foreign languages are:

- French,
- Mandarin,
- German,
- Spanish and
- Arabic.

The acquisition of effective employability skills is significant because as detailed earlier most employers place competence across employability skills above degree subject and degree classification. This is something both school-leavers and graduates should reflect upon when writing CVs and letters of application. Experience and clear evidence of success on a work placement or internship can make up for disappointing exam results or make the difference in competitive interviews. Equally evidence of involvement and participation in projects, events, competitions, community ventures, exchanges, entrepreneurial schemes etc can also provide very valuable evidence of skills development. It is also common for employers to remark that applications and CVs are littered with misspellings, poor grammar and the frustrating attachment of an apostrophe to every plural. This is an issue for graduate recruitment just as much as school leavers. The decline in basic English skills is often charted back to the decision of most major examination boards in the 1990s to cease deducting marks for the poor use of English. Consequently many teachers assumed that poor English should not be corrected and adopted this approach to all written work taking 'teaching to the test' to the extreme. Poor English can, of course, be corrected without deducting marks. The Office for Standards in Education (Ofsted) has included an explicit reference in their current inspection criteria to the importance of teachers correcting English. Ofsted criteria specifies that inspectors will judge, *the monitoring and review of learners' progress in literacy, numeracy, language and key skills, including that work is marked carefully, with correction of spelling, grammatical errors and inaccuracies'.* [17] Consequently all staff should take care to mark for English as well as content but not just to satisfy inspection criteria but because it is a vital skill. In addition the 2010 Government White Paper, *The importance of teaching,* has firmly indicated that examination boards should reconsider their marking policies and return to deducting marks for poor English, *'When young people compete for jobs and enter the workplace, they will be expected to communicate precisely and effectively so we think that changes in the last decade to remove the separate assessment of spelling, punctuation and grammar from GCSE mark schemes were a mistake. We have asked Ofqual to advise on how mark schemes could take greater account of the importance of spelling, punctuation and grammar for examinations in all subjects'.* [18]

World Skills (worldskills.org)

World Skills is essentially the Olympics for vocational courses with students able to compete for Bronze, Silver and Gold awards across 45 vocational areas - anything from Brickwork to Hairdressing. The organisation was founded in 1946 in Spain by Jose Antonio Elola Olas to promote the benefits of vocational education when he was General Director of the Spanish Youth Organisation. The first competition in Spain proved so successful that in 1950 it became an international event and it is now held every two years. The last World Skills championships were held in London October 2011, involving 57 competitor countries, and four British students won prestigious Gold medals as listed in Figure Five:

World skills Gold medal winners[17]
Figure 5

Name	Skill	College
Philip Green	Bricklaying	Belfast Metropolitan
Shane Trevitt	Plumbing and Heating	Leeds College of Building
Christopher Berridge	Stonemasonry	Bath College
Kirsty Hoadley	Visual Merchandising	East Berkshire College

The overall top ten countries in the medal table (ranked by total medal points) were as follows with the UK in fifth position:

1. Korea
2. Japan
3. Switzerland
4. Brazil
5. United Kingdom
6. France

7. Finland
8. Chinese Taipei
9. Australia
10. Austria

It is notable that Asia dominates not just academic league tables but vocational too. Germany appeared in 14th place and the United States of America in 27th place.

The skills wheel[18]

The World Skills definition of generic employability skills takes the form of wheel for visual impact and identifies the following significant skills for entering into self employment.

Figure 6

Enterprise skill wheel

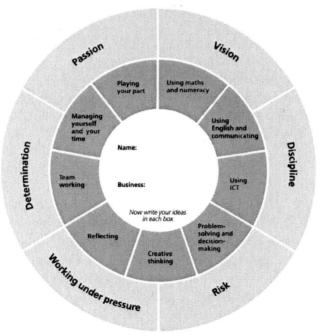

The above skills again confirm the significant themes identified by the Vision 2020, ATC21 and CBI research. Students are invited to work around the wheel and to identify how they might develop and build their personal skills. In addition the theme of self-employment is strongly encouraged by encouraging self-reflection against the following criteria:

Figure 6

Passion	• What idea might I believe in? • How can I believe in myself?
Determination	• How could I show determination every day?
Working under pressure	• What pressures might I face? • How can I overcome them?
Vision	• What vision of success would motivate me to work hard?
Discipline	• When might I need to show discipline • How could I always do my best?
Risk	• What are the risks of starting this business? • How could I make sure these are OK?

The teachers resources linked to the above skills provide very useful prompts to promote discussion and a commitment to building and developing personal and business related skills as well as the students' vocational skills. This awareness raising is an important stepping stone in promoting and establishing the relevance of lessons linked to functional and employability skills to help students to expand their horizons and adopt a broader more holistic view of their abilities rather than a narrow focus on a particular vocational skill or qualification.

A creative framework

There are two significant differences between the skill requirements of the 20th Century and the 21st Century: *Creativity* and *Digital competencies*. The latter as detailed above and defined in the OECD report, '*21st Century Skills and Competences'* highlights the importance of digital competence for all aspects of 21st Century living and working. Creativity however, is perhaps the defining skill for the 21st Century service and hi-tech led economy in terms of the ability to identify problems, find solutions, add value and design new products and services.

Bloom revised

Benjamin Bloom's (1913-99) celebrated cognitive taxonomy was published in 1956 and it has largely withstood critical examination and application. However, during the mid 1990s Lorin W Anderson and David Krathwohl proposed a modification to Bloom's cognitive taxonomy in response to the rise of the Knowledge Age. In 2001 they published, '*A taxonomy for learning, teaching and assessing: A revision of Bloom's taxonomy of educational objectives*'. Their revision partly reordered and renamed Bloom's original taxonomy and substituted verbs for nouns as listed in Figure 7 but its particular contribution was the substitution of *Creating* in place of *Evaluation* as the highest level of cognitive development.

A cognitive taxonomy

Figure 7

Bloom original 1956	Lorin & Krathwohl 2001
Knowledge	Remembering
Comprehension	Understanding
Application	Applying
Analysis	Analysing
Synthesis	Evaluating
Evaluation	Creating

The concept of creativity reflects the opportunities presented by the Knowledge Age as the internet offers the tools and opportunities for ordinary people to turn a craft, invention or hobby into a business or to write an App for a smartphone or to share their music, writing, art, photograph, video or simply musings via a blog or Twitter with the world. The alternatives offered by a Thesaurus to creativity are imaginative, ingenious, inspired, inventive, original, stimulating and visionary. To evaluate is to comment whereas creativity is addition and it is by continuous addition that our knowledge and skills as individuals and a wider society will grow. Consequently creativity must be at the heart of our skills framework but underpinned by digital competencies and competence across wider employability and functional skills. However, what wider skills should schools, colleges and universities foster? Our leading employers have for many decades regularly scoured emerging graduates in so called 'milk rounds' to snap up those with the highest interpersonal, intrapersonal and functional skills. The difference for the 21st Century economy is volume. The switch from an industrial to a service sector based economy has sharply increased demand for many more reliable, IT confident, articulate, numerate and creative workers. Teachers need to respond by integrating regular skills development opportunities across their programmes to ensure that the majority of students develop skills as well as knowledge. However, here terminology becomes problematic and often obscure because there are as many lists of skills as there are organisations and multiple terms in use like key skills, soft skills, employability skills, core skills, essential skills, vocational skills, functional skills, common skills, transferable skills, people skills, world class skills, personal skills etc. Most teachers are bemused and exhausted by this continual re-branding and re-packaging. The answer lies in the overlap i.e. identifying the skills and qualities most frequently agreed as important for personal success and ultimately economic competitiveness.

The common themes, around the core 21st Century skill of creativity, may be expressed as follows:

Skills focus for the 21st Century

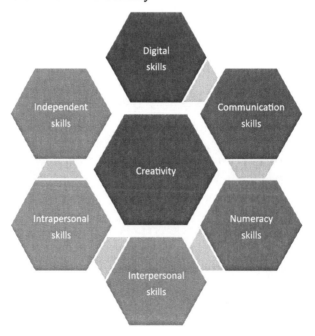

The above skill headings are deliberately broad to permit appropriate interpretation and application by different course teams. However, each theme is significant as indicated by the following descriptors and will hopefully provide a focus for team discussion and the embedding of skills development across all courses.

Figure 8

Skills	Descriptors
Creativity	The skill to identify and resolve problems, design new processes or products, contribute original ideas, vision and add value
Digital	The skill to use and apply digital media and in particular comfort and familiarity with the major functions of Microsoft Office and/or Apple.
Communication	The skill to research, write clear analytical reports, apply standard English and give confident presentations.
Numeracy	The skills to read, interpret, generate and present data and familiarity with mathematical concepts.
Interpersonal	The skills to interact well with others, work in teams, display a positive attitude, persuade and alert to social and cultural differences.
Intrapersonal	The skills to self-assess, reflect, set and manage targets, work to deadlines and know own limitations.
Independent	The skills to independently research, manage and organise own learning and personal development.

Schools and colleges need to further define those broad descriptors and seek consistency of interpretation and application by all teaching staff. In addition, it is important for vocational programmes to identify the major areas of employment targeted by their students and to list the specific skills to succeed and build a satisfying career in those areas of employment? Add in the possibility of future self-employment and further skills will be identified in terms of creativity and entrepreneurship. Once the skills platform has been firmly identified and endorsed by teaching teams there should be regular opportunities to build and develop the desired skill set over the life of the course programme. The development of an online Learning Portal, as described in Chapter Eight, will support the embedding of skills development and creativity and hopefully help to usher in skills as well as knowledge for the 21st Century.

6 A new pedagogy

Today we are failing too many of our children. We're sending them out into a 21st century economy by sending them through the doors of 20th century schools.[1]

Senator Barack Obama 2006

The term pedagogy has unfortunate origins. It arises from the slaves or *Paidagogeos* of Ancient Greece who escorted children to school and armed with a cane beat children who hesitated or got answers wrong or who were deemed to be paying insufficient attention. Essentially a teacher spoke and students listened and learned by rote because there was no alternative way to share or record information. Books, as an alternative source of information, did not appear in significant numbers until the 1500s following the invention of the printing press by Johannes Gutenberg in Hamburg circa 1451. Prior to Gutenberg there were only an estimated 30,000 books in the whole of Europe. However, within fifty years of Gutenberg's invention printers mushroomed across Europe to meet a rising demand for information. Within England William Caxton (1415-92) contributed to this book explosion with the printing of the first book in England, *Recuyell of the History of Troy*, 1473. One of the earliest printers in England was the Oxford University Press (OUP) which printed its first book in 1478 and today is recognised as one of the world's major publishers. By the early 1500s an estimated 8 million books were in print in Europe in what was the world's first information revolution as the words of leading scholars became widely available. Today there are an estimated 130 million unique books in the world and with the ease of self-publishing an e-book an even greater book explosion is on the horizon. Books immediately conferred the ability to learn and to access information independently from a teacher and many ordinary people became expert in a particular field purely from the depth of their personal reading and associated research. There are many examples of amateurs who made discoveries and advanced knowledge without formal lessons in the subject. The power of books to advance learning was recognised in Britain by the passage of the

100

Public Libraries Act 1850 which sought to open libraries in every major town and city to promote a more learned society. The Mechanics Institutes, first formed in 1832, also significantly expanded and offered ordinary workers access to books and opportunities to improve their qualifications. The Board of Education guidance to teachers circa 1904 included the aim …. *to develop in them such a taste for good reading and thoughtful study as will enable them to increase that knowledge in after years by their own efforts".*[2] Consequently the concepts of independent learning and lifelong learning were in vogue long before the computer age. However, there were limitations to this information revolution. Firstly, books were expensive to buy and not everyone had access to a public library. Secondly, not everyone had the skills or motivation to learn independently and thirdly teachers were the gatekeepers of qualifications in terms of interpreting the examination requirements and specifying the key topics to be studied and in what order and to what depth. Most of all, however, the issue was simply one of sufficient access to books and not just any books but finding a 'good' book i.e. sufficient coverage of the relevant course topics. The limited access to books and knowing what to study prevented a more significant learning revolution. Books were largely the preserve of the wealthy and our public libraries carried a limited stock. Those living in cities were best served with books across most major disciplines but less so in our towns and entirely absent in most villages. Interestingly the same issue is evident today in terms of access to a reliable broadband internet service. Students, right up to modern times, used to scour library shelves for a 'good' book and it was a time consuming process. Often it became a question of finding a chapter in a book or scanning the book index to find a single paragraph of relevant information. Whether you found a 'good' book or not was often a question of chance in terms of the selection of books available in your school or local library. More determined scholars might have also scanned publishers' catalogues and requested further books on interlibrary loan and waited for a fortnight for the book to be delivered. Teachers, however, had identified and possessed personal copies of the 'good' books and they extracted from them the key information required for a particular course of study. However, the problem was how to transfer this information to the students in the classroom? The obvious answer returns us full circle to the pedagogy of Ancient Greece. Few schools could afford to buy multiple class sets of the relevant books and so

Online learning

Try entering any of the key topics in your specification (or anything you wish to know) into Google, Ask or Bing and take a look. There will be thousands of hits but within the top rankings you will discover authoritative sources of information from leading institutions, organisations, government(s), charities, businesses, encyclopaedias, museums and academic sites etc. The range of academic resources is ever expanding and among the significant sources for schools and colleges are *thecochranelibrary.com, ebscohost.com, sciencedirect.com, infotrac-college.com, bridgemaneducation.com* and *independence.co.uk/issues-online.* Any professional librarian will probably be able to recommend more and all are excellent gateways to current academic research. How much more might students discover about a topic online compared to what a teacher can present in a one hour lesson? Will the information will be more up-to-date than the class set of textbooks or the teacher's notes gleaned from the 'good' book or remembered from their past university knowledge? Might the students discover a stimulating mix of information across text, photographs video and diagrams? Could they pause and re-read or re-watch or re-examine as wished? Could they also learn at their own pace and study at a time and place of their choosing rather than in a fixed weekly lesson? Most teachers give positive responses to these sorts of questions. In a poll of 600 teachers conducted jointly between the Times Educational Supplement (TES) and the e-Learning Foundation in 2010 68% cited the importance of access to IT in the classroom over traditional teaching materials and over 80% stated that access to the internet at home was either essential or desirable. Internet resources will entirely reshape how we teach and learn because once freed from the need to impart basic factual information teachers can use their lesson time to question, evaluate, analyse and coach students on how to research, validate, present, create and add value. A thesaurus offers the alternative words *'guide'* or *'facilitator'* for a teacher and this perhaps is at the heart of the new pedagogy for the 21st century: the teacher acting as a guide and facilitator of learning. The guide aspect will be significant in terms of identifying and recommending useful resources and in particular useful books. Contrary to popular rumour books are not redundant in the internet age and in fact more are being published than ever before including millions of out-of-print books but as e-books. The Apple app 'Mega Reader' offers over two million free books for an installation cost of £1.49. In 2010 Amazon sold 22 million e-books and now sells more e-books than printed books. The Kobo e-reader linked to WH Smith offers a download choice of 2 million books with one million free books. Google books has three million free books which you can access on any computer, laptop, tablet, smartphone or an e-reader. The books you select are held in your personal library in the Google 'cloud' and you can read them anywhere you have an internet connection. 600 U.S. school districts now issue ipads with digital textbooks as a cost effective alternative to buying and renewing class sets of textbooks. The i-learning pedagogy is expanding rapidly across Higher Education (HE) with the popular *Blackboard.com* Virtual Learning Environment platform. On a wider connected basis the Apple *i-tunes U* (www.apple.com/education/itunes-u) HE service attracts an average of 300 million downloads per year of free university lectures and videos, provided by over 800 universities worldwide. The most popular university materials are provided by the Open University with 40 million downloads in 2010. This is perhaps not too surprising given the OU's reputation for first class independent learning materials (www.open.edu/itunes). The result is that students can access over 350,000 lectures provided by leading academics from most of the world's leading universities like Oxford, Cambridge, Harvard, Stanford, Yale etc without ever setting a foot on campus. Leeds University Medical School has issued a smartphone on loan to all students. The smartphone keeps everyone in contact with course developments via regular texts and a book app provides access to all the required medical textbooks held online. It should also not be forgotten that within the Further Education sector Learn Direct (www.learndirect.co.uk has provided access to online qualifications for over three million students since its inception in 1997. Each month 10,000 students gain a qualification via Learndirect without ever setting foot in a classroom. However, perhaps the simplest but most potent illustration of the i-learning pedagogy in action is the celebrated Khan Academy www.khanacademy.org. The Khan Academy now contains upwards of 2600 short You Tube style videos on a wide variety of key topics and has proved to be immensely popular with over one million views per month. Access is entirely free and for each subject area there is a knowledge tree starting from basic and moving to advanced. Students simply choose their starting position and move forward video by video watching and learning via a step by step presentation of a single 'bite size' chunk of learning. Students re-watch as often as wished because the website never tires of replaying the same video. The system tracks each student's progress and only releases the next level when the one below has been satisfactorily completed. The award of badges up to master level has introduced a competitive gaming environment and encourages students to greater effort to climb the levels. Overall, the availability of reliable online information has reached a tipping point whereby teachers can identify and collate relevant online resources e.g. websites, ebooks, apps, journals, blogs, software for their students to access. Consequently this second information revolution has the power to radically transform our pedagogy by offering students the opportunity to study anywhere and anytime, to work at their own pace, to self-assess their own progress, to collaborate with others, to improve their functional skills and to stimulate and promote their creativity. Enter a primary school classroom and this 21st century learning revolution is already much in evidence.

21st century learning

Suppose the key question in a primary Geography lesson was, *'What is the longest river in the world and its key ecological issues?* In a Twentieth Century classroom the children would have listened while a teacher talked for the whole of several lessons to convey this factual information and/or copied from the board and perhaps referred to a class set of atlases. Some more motivated children might also have visited the library and tried to find a relevant book on the library shelves. Today in the 21st century Generation Z merely put the question into Google, Bing or Ask. The response in less than a split second is 4,810,000 hits but the first 15 or so are all excellent authoritative sources with full and detailed answers to the question. The first hit displays a table of the 25 longest rivers in the world and the answer (not the one you were thinking of) is the Nile which is 4,135 miles long. The Amazon is in second place at 3,980 miles. Interestingly the third hit on Google is the Virtual Learning Environment (VLE) of Woodlands Junior School in Kent UK where the children have completed a project on rivers and everything you would wish to know about major world rivers including their ecology complete with video and photographs is there to read and download. Generation Z might then visit Google Earth and follow the length of the Nile by satellite and if wished call up live web cameras along its

In-House Training
604c Huddersfield Road, Ravensthorpe
Dewsbury WF13 3HL
01924 500647
www.ihtlearning.co.uk
Vat Number 981 981 175   Com Reg 07512521

route to view real time pictures. They might also find and email schools in the region and ask direct questions of other children about their lives and interact via a video link. Their questions might lead to investigating how best to provide clean drinking water and link to science to explore current technology and development projects and perhaps fundraising for a relevant charity. Finally, they might choose to present their findings in a short publication, a podcast, a video, a photo slideshow or a direct presentation supported by Powerpoint, Keynote or Prezi. This interactive learning is highly engaging, develops individual skills, builds knowledge and leads to creativity. Learners who are regularly involved in individual, paired and group activities to research and present core information will also develop the interpersonal, intrapersonal, research and creative skills valued by the hi- tech and service sectors of the 21st Century economy. This rich online world of learning is the present not the future. Longfield Academy in Kent hit the headlines in September 2011 by becoming the first High School in England to issue ipads to all pupils. Will Generation Z be content to sit still in straight rows when they reach your High School or your College classroom and listen for most of the lesson and copy down lots of notes from the board or as you talk? How many might be tempted to defy the rules and switch on the smartphone in their pocket and find the information? Rather than our students being passive recipients of information we are drawing them into being active participants. The future is one of continuous updating, exploring and shifting our focus from the teacher as the sole source of information to the multiple information resources of the internet and drawing upon peers, friends, family and the wider community i.e. promoting and facilitating independent or more simply i-learning.

The hole-in-the-wall

The success of even unsupported self-access to the internet was demonstrated by the Hole-in-the-Wall project in India (www.hole-in-the-wall.com). In 1999 the Chief Scientist of the IT company NIIT (www.niit.com) Dr. Sugata Mitra placed a computer in a hole-in-a-wall in the Kalkaji slum district of New Delhi and watched. Within weeks the children had taught themselves how to use the computer and to access the internet and by the end of the project the children had:

- Become computer literate on their own to the standard of an average lay user,
- Taught themselves enough English to use email, chat and search engines,
- Discovered how to search the internet for answers to questions,
- mproved their English pronunciation,
- Improved their mathematics and science scores in school,
- Answered examination questions several years ahead of their time,
- Improved their social interaction skills,
- Formed independent opinions and questioned indoctrination.

Today there is a hole-in-the-wall computer in 300 locations across India and the concept is spreading to other countries in what Mitra has dubbed, 'minimally invasive education'.

Log-in

Many of our schools and colleges have benefited from bright, new buildings which are fully 'wired' and reflect the support requirements of the digital age. However, whether old or new the key is a Wifi campus to permit staff and students to log-in from any position and in particular from regular 'open spaces' i.e. in addition to large central Learning Centres clusters of chairs and tables for individuals and small groups to log-in across the campus taking advantage of any open space including outdoor seating. Take down walls if need be to open up space and post examples of role models, student successes, sports successes, exam successes, self-employment and career suggestions, local and world citizenship involvement etc to promote an opportunity rich environment. Perhaps brand such open spaces as Learning Pods and in the case of any concern about poor behaviour in such open and informal settings ensure the extension and prominent siting of CCTV coverage. All students should be online at college and as far as possible at home. In terms of the latter colleges and schools should know how many students do not have a home computer and/or home broadband. The educational advantage of having books at home is well known with the possession of around 200+ books correlating with higher than average achievement. Access to the internet is perhaps even more important given the ease of access to not only books but a wealth of wider information sources. The significant disparity between low and high income households in terms of access to both books and the internet is highlighted by the percentages in Figure 1 provided by the Organisation for Economic Co-operation and Development (OECD).[3] The percentages are an average across OECD member states 2010 and demonstrate a close correlation between the possession of books and the internet. Whether it is access to books or the internet some students are placed at a learning disadvantage and schools and colleges need to reach out to parent(s) and guardians(s) to offer advice and guidance on how best to support learning.

Home internet access

Figure 1

Home access	Low income household	High income household
Text Books	75%	96%
Internet	72%	97%

An option for schools and colleges is to purchase and lease computers or tablets like the ipad to students to ensure that they all have access to at least a computer at home. This is often beyond the means of schools or colleges with limited budgets to administer but the e-Learning Foundation charity (www.e-learningfoundation.com) is dedicated to helping to manage access to computers and the internet. The Foundation offers expert guidance and can manage leasing arrangements and provide grants for the purchase of computers. Access to the internet is more difficult to resolve for those without a home broadband connection and students in this situation will have to seek and take advantage of free Wifi hotspots or to adopt the study habit of arriving early or staying late to access the college or school service. Advantage might also be taken of local libraries, community centres and any college or school local outreach centres. If access remains problematic then each course should issue a memory stick loaded with the relevant handouts, textbooks, video etc so that students with a computer but no internet connection can access the core learning materials at home. All online students should be encouraged to take up the free 'cloud' space on offer by Google or Amazon and many other providers so that they access and work on the same version of their assignments rather than the confusion of holding multiple versions on memory sticks, laptops and computers. Alternatively your school or college server may have sufficient capacity to grant personal file space. South Korea already maintains a public Wifi network and has set 2015 as the target date to equip all students with tablets and for the conversion of all school textbooks to e-books to be held on a dedicated 'education cloud'. New York has designated an izone for linking all of its schools online. The steady expansion of online resources will significantly boost learning by extending learning opportunities beyond the classroom.

The i-learning pedagogy

The concept of learning a subject within the confines of 3 or 4 weekly timetabled lessons can and will disappear as reliable online resources proliferate. With Wifi access to the internet learning can spill over the edges of timetabled lessons into the physical 'open spaces' across our campuses and into the open spaces of spare time in our days, evenings and weekends. We can learn anywhere and anytime. Most of our students have broadband at home, a smartphone in their pocket and increasingly a laptop or a tablet computer. Consequently the core curriculum focus will shift from classroom and teaching to the Individual Learning Plan (ILP) and learning.

Press any key to continue...

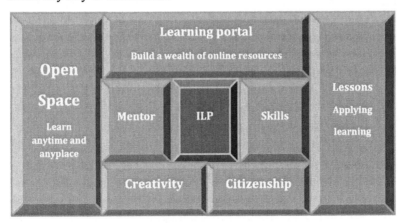

At the heart of an i-learning pedagogy is the Individual Learning Plan (ILP) and preferably an electronic ILP which sets manageable but challenging learning goals. The traffic light system of green, yellow and red is perhaps one of the most effective at-a-glance assessment systems to prompt progress. The ILP should ideally be placed online and open to all relevant staff to view and update and equally accessible by parent(s) and guardian(s) of students aged under 18 years. This instant source of shared information should also facilitate communication between schools and colleges for 14-16 programmes and in particular to monitor attendance. There is an absolute correlation between attendance and achievement and any slippage should be rigorously acted upon. Although our definition of attendance should shift to include logged-on i.e. logged-on to the College or school Virtual Learning Environment (VLE). The progress of every student should be closely monitored by a Learning Mentor who can offer a listening ear and aim to monitor and support all aspects of each student's progress. The mentor should check and prompt progress, identify blocks to progress and intervene with additional support as required to ensure the completion of agreed study targets. All students thrive when they feel a sense of belonging, recognition and support and contact by email and text straight to the students' mobile phones should be standard in addition to one to one and group mentor sessions.

Redefining teaching

The new pedagogy of online resources and independent learning will redefine teachers and teaching in three significant ways:
Teachers will be less defined by their subject knowledge and more by their ability to facilitate online learning, to build learning skills and to

Facilitation	Skills focus	learning focus
• building a learning portal • identifying useful online resources • warning against unreliable resources • highlighting current research / developments • adding own videos and resources	• coaching search skills • teaching independent learning skills • moving beyond horizontal research • avoiding the trap of 'cut and paste' • using Microsoft Office and/or Apple software	• setting and monitoring learning targets • updating ILP • lessons with regular individual, paired and group tasks • more one to one • developing Functional and employability skills

coach and support the progress of each individual. The result will be a 'flipped learning' environment as learning moves online and the 'flip' to an i-learning pedagogy will hopefully address Obama's spur to reform as quoted at the start of this chapter.

110

Flipped learning

> "Self-education should be the key-note of the older children's curriculum...instruction will only have it fullest effect when the teacher realises that his chief task is to teach the scholars to teach themselves, and adapt his methods steadily to that end'. [1]
>
> Board of Education, Handbook for Teachers, first printed 1904.

A common approach to teaching and learning is to use lesson time for 'chalk and talk' to describe and explain key topic information which pupils or students record as notes (teaching) and to use homework to set questions or tasks to promote a deeper reflection, analysis and evaluation of the topic information (learning). However, the latter is more demanding and it is common for most pupils and students to experience difficulties and misunderstandings with homework tasks. Without a teacher at home to help most will ask their siblings, parents and/or their friends for help. The problem is so common that the BBC Radio Two, 'Drive Time' programme has a feature entitled 'homework sucks' to help listeners to complete their homeworks. Most pupils or students find homework tasks difficult because they are analysing and evaluating information. In contrast the classroom often raises fewer demands because the focus is largely on note-taking from teacher 'chalk and talk', a textbook or watching video etc. Flipped learning 'flips' the less demanding note-taking tasks out of the classroom to form the homework task and reserves the classroom for a mixture of individual, paired and group tasks to discuss and apply the topic information with the added advantage of teacher support.

The concept of flipped learning arose in 2007 from an innovative experiment by Jonathan Bergmann and Aaron Sams who were both teachers at Woodlands Park High School in Woodlands, Colorado. Bergmann and Sams videoed their lessons to help students who had missed the lessons to catch-up. The videos proved popular but in a significant addition Bergman and Sams produced 'advance' videos of future classroom topics and invited the students to watch the

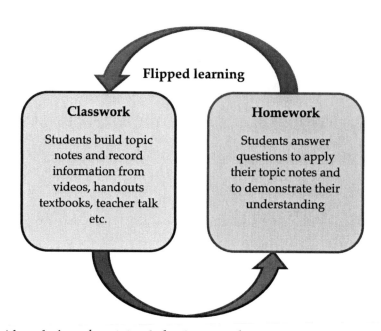

Flipped learning

Classwork

Students build topic notes and record information from videos, handouts textbooks, teacher talk etc.

Homework

Students answer questions to apply their topic notes and to demonstrate their understanding

videos before they joined the lesson. The videos permitted the students to absorb the basic facts online and when they entered the classroom they tended to have questions and the lesson time became more devoted to discussion and less to imparting basic facts. The students also gained the opportunity to re-watch as they wished and to learn at their own pace anytime and anywhere and all gradually shifted from being passive listeners to active participants. The key benefit for both teachers was gaining more time to focus on coaching and building higher order thinking and reasoning skills and answering students' questions. Consequently far from being redundant the flipped learning model needs teachers more than ever to apply their subject expertise to identify and resolve student misunderstandings, to support and stretch each student and to target the achievement of high grades. Although the term 'homework' is used in the above diagram in practice it refers to engaging in independent learning outside of the classroom whether at home, school, college, local library etc and using resources placed by the teacher on the school or college Virtual Learning Environment (VLE) for ease of access. The resources can include a core of recommended videos sourced from the internet, personally produced videos, ebooks, websites, handouts etc. The online reading and research is steered by setting key questions and with encouragement to conduct a wider webquest. A bridge task at the ends of lessons can be used to issue a 'bridge' question or task as the key focus for the next lesson and over the course of several lessons to systematically explore and absorb all of the recommended resources for a particular topic. A common reaction to the concept of flipped learning is concern that too many students will fail to complete the advance online reading and note-taking tasks and arrive at their lessons ill-prepared. However, the non-completion of homeworks by a minority of pupils or students is not a new issue and the response should be the same. A repeated failure to complete advance reading and note-taking tasks may highlight a need for some students to receive extra study skills support or behaviour management intervention and appropriate strategies are discussed and provided in Chapter Nine. However, as the advance tasks are largely note-taking from specified resources, along with encouragement to conduct a wider web quest, all should be able to manage and will hopefully enjoy and gain motivation by exploring the mix of resources. Within the classroom those who have completed their advance reading and note-taking can engage with individual, paired and group tasks to deepen their learning and those who have not completed the advance task can be directed to the Learning Centre to complete the necessary reading and note-taking. Once flipped learning is introduced the 20th century classroom of a teacher standing at the front with largely passive students seated in straight rows listening will give way to the 21st century classroom of participative learning with the teacher circulating, prompting, listening, explaining and questioning.

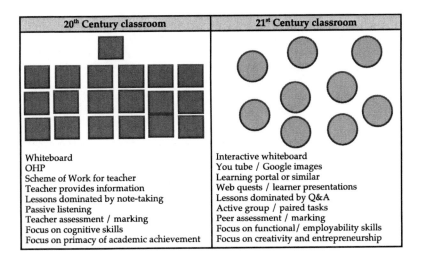

20th Century classroom	21st Century classroom
Whiteboard OHP Scheme of Work for teacher Teacher provides information Lessons dominated by note-taking Passive listening Teacher assessment / marking Focus on cognitive skills Focus on primacy of academic achievement	Interactive whiteboard You tube / Google images Learning portal or similar Web quests / learner presentations Lessons dominated by Q&A Active group / paired tasks Peer assessment / marking Focus on functional/ employability skills Focus on creativity and entrepreneurship

The significant advantage of flipped learning is that the teacher is in the classroom and able to respond to questions as they arise, to help students to resolve any misunderstandings or misconceptions as they apply their research and compare their note-taking with other students in regular individual, paired and group tasks. This will promote much deeper learning because the students will have had time to reflect upon their note-taking and will have questions and be aware of aspects they do not fully understand. In contrast in standard 'chalk and talk' lessons, students are expected to immediately respond to and question new information as it is presented. The involvement in paired and group discussions will also promote peer learning because students will often ask questions of each other that they would not ask in front of a whole class and confidence will grow when they discover that someone else shares the same misunderstanding. To facilitate beneficial exchanges the students should be placed into regular mixed ability groups or pairs to encourage peer questioning and peer teaching. Deeper and more productive learning will result because peer working extends and challenges individual assumptions.

Applying Bloom's Taxonomy

Flipped learning maintains the importance of moving from 'lower order' to 'higher order' thinking and reasoning skills as specified by Bloom's Taxonomy and Piagetian programmes. Bloom's taxonomy, as described in Chapter Five, was revised in 2001 by Anderson &

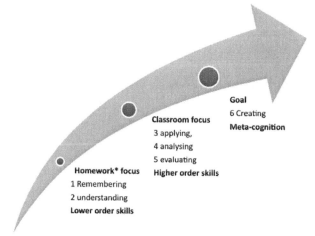

Goal
6 Creating
Meta-cognition

Classroom focus
3 applying,
4 analysing
5 evaluating
Higher order skills

Homework* focus
1 Remembering
2 understanding
Lower order skills

* The term homework is used for convenience and is defined as any independent learning tasks undertaken outside of the classroom.

Krathwohl to reflect the demands of 21st century employment and the six steps from remembering to the highest cognitive function of creating are illustrated above in relation to the flipped learning model. The ultimate goal of creativity and meta-cognition is built upon a firm foundation of developing the capacity for independent learning and raising the ability to self-question and identify own support needs

Lessons with soft edges

The 'flipped' lesson has soft edges which overlap with online learning beyond the classroom to end the concept of learning within a fixed time in a fixed room. This is not new because independent learners have always continued learning outside of the classroom, but our significant goal is to prompt and support the majority of our students to follow their example. There is an obvious and high correlation between time spent studying and achievement rates and by gaining regular independent learning outside of the classroom we can double or treble learning time. The concern that many teachers express of insufficient time to cover the curriculum will recede as online learning provides additional and more extensive learning opportunities. Lesson and course planning should focus more on topics than individual lessons and plan for the best mix of teaching and learning experiences across the full span of the time allocated to each topic both in and outside the classroom. The Learning Portal described in Chapter Eight highlights how resources might be structured on the Virtual Learning Environment by topic and linked to individual lessons. The aim should be to be creative with lesson time and to move beyond whole classes meeting every lesson into a wider mix of classroom experiences as follows:

- Setting key questions to guide independent reading and research.
- Placing recommended resources on the Learning Portal or similar.
- Delivering a whole class lecture style presentation (appropriate for some courses) to provide an overview but planned and delivered as a lecture with full visual, questioning and handout support.

- Inviting a visiting speaker to present up-to-date information (may be a colleague to add a different view or specialist input) The students should prepare questions to ask.
- Facilitating planned student presentations of their research and findings,
- Encouraging informal student presentations arising from in-class group tasks
- Extending peer learning via a joint lesson with a parallel class
- Extending peer learning via a joint lesson with a different year group
- Providing one to one support while the rest of class are logged-in to the learning portal or engaged in paired or group tasks.
- Providing small group coaching support while the rest of the class are logged-in to the learning portal or engaged in paired or group tasks,
- Subdividing the lesson time into short 15 to 20 minute 'bite size' chunk presentations to explain answers to key questions. Perhaps three or four in response to student feedback. Permit the students to opt in or out.
- Designating some whole lessons as 'Recap' to review and consolidate key learning
- Designating some whole lessons as 'Accelerate' to advance learning to address the highest grades / performance
- Devoting a whole lesson to a focus on individual and/or paired tasks – peer working
- Devoting a whole lesson to a group task – peer working in mixed ability groups.

Essentially the lessons are reserved for activities to check and consolidate learning and understanding with the Learning Portal as the primary source of core topic information. Check that the students regularly log-in to access the core topic information in the 'open spaces' of the school or college between lessons and at home. Key lessons might be repeated at different times during the week in the spirit of 'catch-up' TV and offered by different teachers for students to join. Capture any 'bite size' 10 or 15 minute presentations on video and place on the Learning Portal or VLE and overtime build your own collection and/or upload to the teacher zone of You Tube. Overall focus on the achievement of the learning outcomes for the topic i.e. what the students should know and be able to explain rather

116

than simply 'coverage' of topic information and identify and focus on those who need further support. The relationship between teacher and student(s) is very different and more productive on a one to one or in small groups compared to a whole class and significant advances can be made in terms of reforming attitudes and identifying and resolving individual barriers to progress. This task centred approach to learning resolves many of the issues of classroom behaviour management because it leads to greater engagement and a sense of choice and personal responsibility to learn. Consequently our recording of attendance should be adjusted to include logged-in as well as physically present in a classroom to shift our focus to task completion rather than being seated in a classroom. Overall learning is in fast transition as the online world expands and many teachers as well as students will need support to leave the 20th century classroom behind.

Re-arrange your classroom

To reflect the wider mix of classroom activities the classroom furniture should be regularly re-arranged to sharpen the focus on the task. Consequently, as far as possible equip all classrooms with interactive whiteboards, flipcharts and small individual desks for easy reconfiguration. Move and re-arrange the desks to suit the different learning tasks:

- Straight rows theatre style to watch a DVD or a whole class presentation,
- Two facing straight rows to facilitate a debate,
- One large central block for a whole group discussion,
- Small clusters of desks for small group activity,
- A few individual spaced desks with no chairs for three or maximum of four students to stand around to brainstorm a task (we can say brainstorm).
- Two or three blocks of desks for team work.
- A single hot seat in the centre of the room preferably a swivel chair and the rest of the chairs in a circle ready to question the person in the hot seat – (teachers as well as students) on prepared topics
- A horseshoe arrangement to encourage discussion
- A circle without desks to encourage sharing of opinions

The above examples illustrate how the physical repositioning of the furniture directs attention to the task with sometimes just a single learning focus for a whole lesson. The alternative is that students will often sit beside the same person at the same desk every lesson and quickly fall into a 'comfort zone'. Sitting in the same position every lesson can also lead to the formation of sub-groups which can isolate some students and confirm adopted or 'allocated' roles within the lesson e.g. class clown, swot, troublemaker, silent, shy etc. The regular re-arrangement of furniture linked to paired and group tasks will disturb those behaviours / labels and overtime stimulate a focus on the task and spark greater engagement. In addition regular mixing will build and sustain a co-operative bond of mutual support and build a learning dialogue and full participation between the students and their teacher(s).

A learning dialogue

Successful learning dialogues are more commonly observed within vocational workshops rather than theory lessons because the students become fully engaged and absorbed by the practical tasks. The students know exactly what they have to do and apply themselves while the teacher circulates and checks progress and delivers timely interventions to coach improvements. This is participative learning in action with students seeking guidance, asking questions and the teachers facilitating, guiding and coaching. The sequence of learning may have high teacher direction but in operation it is also fully participative:

- explain the task,
- show exemplars,
- demonstrate the skill,
- monitor progress,
- ask students to explain their progress in terms of difficulty or understanding,
- correct misunderstandings as they arise,
- offer individual coaching,
- provide small group coaching,
- encourage peer coaching / collaboration,
- issues words of praise / recognition,
- invite self-assessment against standards or exemplars

The majority of students thrive in this active learning environment because of the clarity of the tasks, the unambiguous success criteria and in particular because they are conscious of real improvements to their skills. They know what they can now do and this awareness builds self-belief which translates into higher motivation and ultimately greater effort.

There are many highly successful 14-16 school-college vocational partnerships which fully engage young people. Flipped learning essentially imports into the theory classroom the successful learning sequence of the vocational workshop by opening up opportunities for teacher circulation and individual coaching as the students work in pairs and groups. The outcomes of regular paired and group tasks should be displayed on 'learning walls' in our classrooms and this can be extended onto the VLE with the addition of student created Powerpoints, photoslide shows, podcasts, video etc. Overtime ensure that all students have some of their work displayed because it will build confidence and pride in tasks well-completed and drive higher standards once students are aware that their work will be on public display.

Flexible support and guidance

The focus on independent learning outside of the classroom highlights the need for learning support to be spread much more widely than individual teachers. The learner should be encouraged to seek support from others both within and outside the college or school as illustrated to help extend their learning.

Within the college or school a rota of mentors and learning support staff, skilled in Microsoft Office applications, should circulate around the 'open spaces' and Learning Centres to provide coaching support as required. This type of informal support is highly beneficial because it is provided at the point of need, while students are busy working on assignments, and offers a 'pull' rather than a 'push' relationship. The regular circulation of staff also deters inappropriate behaviour. The mentor is the key person to monitor progress and to offer learning support but with an enquiry based curriculum (regularly answering key questions and completing Webquests) students may seek support not only from their mentors but also other support staff, Learning Centre staff, wider family, parent(s), guardian(s), neighbours, charitable organisations, faith groups and community volunteers who may be able to coach or help provide support. Parent(s) in particular can make a major difference and they should be welcomed as equal partners in helping to promote learning, career and university opportunities and to play an active part in the life of the school or college with regular suggestions on how to get involved. School or college websites should have a parent or guardian log-in to course information pages to provide information on key learning targets and how best they might help their son or daughter to learn. The gain will hopefully be a beneficial 'push' from home. To facilitate wider support and 'flipped learning' all schools and colleges should consider the development of a 'learning portal' or similar to *drive* rather than just support learning.

8 The Learning Portal

"Give a man a fish and you feed him for a day; teach a man to fish and you feed him for a lifetime".

Old English proverb, author unknown

The traditional A4 Scheme of Work grid, employed by most of our schools and colleges, is perhaps redundant in the internet era and should be abandoned and recast an integral part of the school or college Virtual Learning Environment (VLE). Teachers will gain much more professional satisfaction from building an online learning programme and students will gain immediate study guidance and support within a 'click and go' learning environment. An electronic scheme of work with linked access to recommended resources will also advance independent learning anywhere and anytime. Students who are recovering from illness in hospital or at home, or away on work placements or field trips, or trips abroad or extended holiday will all be able to continue learning within minimum interruption. Equally cover for absent teachers is made much easier. However, in too many schools and colleges the Virtual Learning Environment (VLE) lacks structure and operates in isolation from the Scheme of Work and classroom. It is common to enter a VLE, click on a subject heading and find that all that exists to support learning is a blank space for the attachment of resources e.g. handouts, Powerpoints, web site recommendations etc. Many staff do respond and upload resources but the result is all too often a random collection of folders rather than a guided pathway through useful topic linked resources. VLEs should avoid becoming repositories for files or a source of extended learning or an electronic filing cabinet for replacement copies of lost handouts etc. The VLE should be the focal point to *drive* rather than *support* learning and this requires a more structured layout and an underpinning pedagogy to link the classroom and learning to the VLE. To lead learning an electronic VLE based Scheme of Work should:

- Identify each major topic,

- Attach recommended resources to each major topic
- Link lessons to each topic
- Specify short-term targets with clear learning goals
- Provide differentiated self-check key questions to prompt self-assessment
- Encourage involvement in a Q&A forum to facilitate peer/teacher support
- Integrate employability skills across research and presentation based tasks
- Offer extended learning and challenge tasks
- Specify the core (minimum) subject knowledge all should know

An exemplar electronic Scheme of Work, entitled 'Learning Portal' which demonstrates how all of these features might be integrated into a VLE is provided on the Collegenet website (collegenet.co.uk).

Learning Portal

The Collegenet Learning Portal employs web based software and is essentially three interlinked web pages to offer students full topic by topic support. Essentially the Portal should become the primary learning focus and underpin all learning within and beyond the classroom. The recommended 'flipped learning' pedagogy (see Chapter Seven) is for students to absorb core subject and topic information from the specified online resources and to use the resources to prepare for classroom discussion and wider individual, paired and group tasks. The students are encouraged to learn anytime and anyplace and to take greater responsibility for their own learning and to appreciate that learning does not just happen within a timetabled lesson. This strategy will liberate both teachers and students from the slow transfer of factual information within the classroom and should permit most of the class-time to be reserved for more productive discussion and for question and answer to help to analyse and evaluate the core topic information. The obvious flaw in this strategy is the students! Not all of our students possess effective independent learning skills. However, this raises a significant teaching function to coach, support and develop the necessary study and organisational skills and this is addressed in Chapter Nine.

In-House Training
604c Huddersfield Road, Ravensthorpe
Dewsbury WF13 3HL
01924 500647
www.ihtlearning.co.uk
Vat Number 981 981 175   Com Reg 07512521

Learning Portal home page

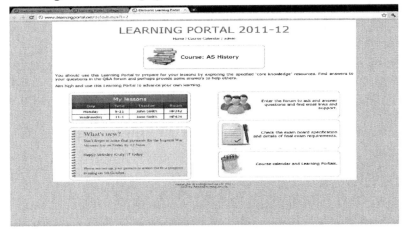

The above screen shot of the Portal *home page* is faint and so do please visit Collegenet.co.uk to view a clickable live version. Most VLEs offer students some form of home page to support learning and a wide variety of features and support options can be included. In this exemplar the features are:

- A subject timetable
- A 'what's new' notepad
- A link to an online Question and Answer forum
- A link to examination information
- A link to the course calendar for an at-a-glance overview of the course programme.

The subject timetable confirms the basic lesson arrangements. The *'What's new'* notepad is a virtual noticeboard to highlight events, deadlines, instructions or even personal greetings with the example here, *'happy birthday Kirsty 17th today'*. Question and Answer forums tend to be standard features of VLEs but here attention is drawn to the free resources for closed group accounts offered by both Google and Facebook. In either case individual teachers can open accounts and sign-in their class as a closed private membership. Facebook, in particular, may be more attractive because many students maintain a Facebook account and will be immediately familiar with its style and functionality. A Q&A forum offers all students an immediate source of support but to be effective as a learning tool the Q&A forum needs to be integrated into the lessons. Simply inviting students to use a

Q&A forum will have limited impact. Teachers should post key questions, linked to the lesson, in the Q&A Forum and regularly enter the Forum during lessons to check open discussions, to set fresh questions and to invite answers within a specified deadline. The teacher should prompt deeper responses, extend answers, praise answers and follow-up any evidence of particular misunderstandings as part of a lesson recap or discussion. In this way the Q&A forum becomes a live tool to promote participation and deeper learning rather than an occasional recommendation that many students may choose to ignore. The Portal also provides a link to the examination specification to ensure that all students have access to the formal examination requirements. Key paragraphs should be highlighted and referred to in class to reinforce the standards expected and to encourage the students to read and apply the specification standards. The final link on the home page is to a *course calendar* and this presents an 'at-a-glance' overview of the academic year from September to July or the relevant timescale. A column is provided for the teacher to list the major topics in their recommended order of study. The topics are entered against the relevant week dates so that the programme is very clear and the depth of study is reflected in the number of weeks allocated to each topic. Alongside the topic list is a parallel column to list significant course events progress evenings, career events, charitable fundraising events, sporting events, visiting speaker, trips etc. This column should highlight a variety of opportunities and stimulating events across the academic year and if left blank should prompt the course team to consider how far the course programme is providing sufficient stretch and challenge. All students need something to look forward to and so hopefully there will be an appropriate mix of fun and motivational events as well as more formal course related activities.

The portal

The cover of this textbook illustrates the Portal and as repeated below. Essentially each topic, listed by a teacher on the Calendar Page, has its own portal as illustrated. This ensures an explicit topic by topic structure to the provision of online resources and will support the less confident and less skilled students to find and access the key recommended resources.

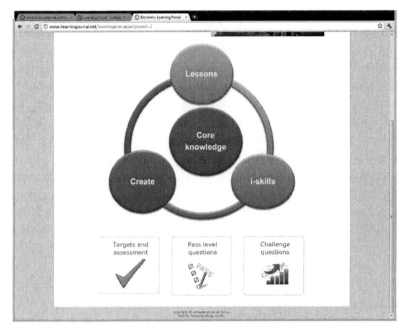

The portal is deliberately highly visual to stimulate interest and to offer consistency of approach by different teaching staff so that the learning support on offer is uniform and students can build familiarity and confidence of navigation. It represents a balance between being overly extensive and not comprehensive enough. The portal prompts effective practice in teaching and learning across self-assessment, short term learning goals, metacognition, assessment for learning, creativity, independent study, differentiation, embedding employability / functional skills and underpins the development of a 'flipped learning' environment.

Core knowledge

Students are first invited to enter the Core Knowledge to explore resources to support the relevant topic. The resources might include an e-book, a periodical article, a video, relevant websites, photographs, a podcast, a biography, key charts and statistics, Powerpoint, maps, a blog, a handout, a worksheet, a TV programme etc. Teachers should upload the resources created to support each topic in the normal course of lesson preparation rather than any significant extra demand and over time draw from the internet and perhaps add own videos and student generated learning materials. The availability of software like Camtasia permits teachers to record their 'chalk and talk' narration as short, sharp videos linked to key Powerpoint or Keynote slides. To help build the Learning Portal teachers should end each lesson ten minutes early and use the ten minutes to upload the learning resources used in the lesson. This will steadily populate the Learning Portal over an academic year and offer the students in the following year(s) the opportunity for advance learning topic by topic. If more than one teacher teaches a course then collaboration is the way forward with each teacher undertaking a topic and uploading the resources for all to share. On a larger scale many schools and colleges operate within consortiums and they could pool their resources and collectively develop and refine a common Learning Portal. Most colleges and schools also have well-resourced libraries or Learning Centres staffed by information specialists who can help to recommend and populate the Portal with useful resources and ensure that relevant websites, periodicals and textbooks etc. are not overlooked. This close involvement of Learning Centre staff will build closer links between the support offered by the Learning Centre and the classroom to build a seamless learning environment. The students will gain significantly by absorbing the Core Knowledge resources at their own speed and in their own time and be in a better position to engage in classroom discussion and wider learning tasks.

Lessons

The clickable link to lessons within the portal encourages teaching staff to specify a short, sharp summary of the learning focus for each lesson. This clarity of purpose goes to the heart of effective teaching and learning because it will facilitate 'real-time' checks on learning during and at the ends of lessons. This focus could be further sharpened by listing key questions to guide the students' research and as a focus for classroom discussion and answer. With the advance exploration of the Core Knowledge resources most students will enter the lessons with questions and the lesson will become much more interactive with the teacher in a coaching role and using most of the lesson time for individual, paired and group tasks to check and extend understanding. What have the students discovered? What do they know and importantly what do they misunderstand? This approach will facilitate deep rather than surface learning and assist all to apply their knowledge to best of their abilities.

Individual skills (i-skills)

As identified in Chapter Five there are six significant areas of skills development for future living and working in the 21st century:

- *Digital competencies*
- *Communication – written and oral*
- *Numeracy and core mathematical functions*
- *Interpersonal skills*
- *Intrapersonal skills*
- *Independent skills i.e. learning to learn*

The development of competency across these skills will be vital for all individuals and just as important to employers as the knowledge of a particular subject. Consider how often an employer will ask an employee to explain the differences between Sole Traders and Limited Companies compared to how often they will ask an employee to analyse a spreadsheet, summarise a report, design a powerpoint, telephone a customer, write a report, write a letter etc. Any course that develops subject knowledge alone without developing skills should be challenged because it is not preparing young people for the realities of future university and/or employment. Highlight the importance of these skills for future living and working by including a skills development objective or practice opportunity as one of your lesson objectives. Make the skills visible. This section of the Portal should detail individual, paired and/or group tasks planned for the lesson or for completion outside the classroom with appropriate deadlines. The tasks should all draw upon the Core Knowledge resources and carry forward the learning objectives by permitting time for reflection, deeper research and the consolidation of the key knowledge. The completion of the tasks should also be designed to offer practice opportunities to build employability and Functional Skills over time and lesson by lesson rather than Functional Skills being associated with a weekly timetabled lesson. Every teacher is a teacher of employability and Functional Skills and regular tasks lesson by lesson will build competence and confidence across Communication, Number and ICT in particular. The activities to engage students in learning might include:

- Researching online
- Reading textbooks or handouts
- Reading a blog
- Reading periodicals
- Reading and analysing tables of statistics
- Creating tables of statistics
- Adding, subtracting, calculating percentages etc
- Placing data into a chart
- Using a spreadsheet
- Creating a database
- Categorising and sorting information
- Examining website resources
- Using software
- Playing competitive learning games
- Taking notes for many different sources
- Watching a video
- Designing a Powerpoint or Keynote presentation
- Designing a Prezi presentation
- Recording a short video
- Designing a poster
- Designing a factsheet
- Conducting an experiment
- Conducting a survey
- Interviewing people
- Vocabulary and definitions checklists and spelling tests
- Creating timelines
- Role playing a relevant encounter
- Writing a short, sharp definition or answer
- Writing an essay
- Writing to a time limit
- Writing a blog
- Writing a report
- Writing a long assignment
- Collating a portfolio
- Taking photographs
- Creating a photo slideshow
- Uploading information onto the VLE or internet
- Downloading information from the VLE or internet
- Designing a questionnaire
- Creating a podcast

- Giving a presentation
- Holding opinions in a debate
- Making something
- Completing a test to a time limit
- Demonstrating a process or equipment
- Creating a display
- Resolving a case study with a solution
- Leading a group
- Explaining something you know well to someone else
- Posing questions
- Drawing a spider diagram or visual representations
- Mind mapping a topic

Apply your own creativity and consider carefully the skill needs of the relevant vocational area or the future employment prospects of your students and ensure that this section of the Portal includes tasks designed to practice and build the relevant skills.

Create

Living and working in the 21st Century is all about creativity as the internet opens a myriad of ways for self-expression. A simple blog, photograph, tweet, video, program, game, drawing, sketch, lecture, joke, dance, book, app, cartoon, gadget, poem, song, invention etc can suddenly take-off and capture attention and interest once it circulates on the internet. Or in the language of the age goes viral. Work experience placements can stimulate creativity if students are invited to consider improvements to customer service, production methods etc. Ask the question 'what improvements might you make? The Sixth Form student Hannah Blyth has an asteroid named after her following a work experience placement with astronomers at the University of Glamorgan in 2011. Hannah spotted an unknown and uncharted asteroid between Mars and Jupiter and it has been formally recorded and named Hannah-Blyth in honour of her discovery. The Physics students of Langton Grammar School in Canterbury under the direction of Dr Becky Parker the Head of Physics have beaten Nasa to developing a detector for cosmic radiation. Dr Parker despairs of science experiments which are not experiments because the answer you should get is invariably recorded in the textbook. When is an experiment not an experiment?

Our future prosperity in terms of the development of hi-tech industry and services relies upon skilled employees or ordinary individuals who identify improvements to processes, systems and products or who can shape an idea and develop it. Creativity can be interpreted in its widest sense of individual endeavour and may be as simple as encouraging contributions to community organisations, fundraising for a charity, young enterprise activity, participating in drama, music, sport or any wider enrichment activity to help to raise horizons and extend individuals beyond their day to day routine. It is also important to encourage self-employment because with the internet it has never been easier to set up a small business with very low overheads and minimal start-up costs. One college catering department regularly gives their students £10 each with the challenge to return a profit to stir their entrepreneurial skills and ambitions. The organisation *I am creative* links industry with schools and colleges to undertake real creative projects for real products or events at www.iamcreative.org.uk. Emma Rushin won a £50,000 prize from Walker's Crisps in 2008 for her suggestion of Builder's Breakfast crisps as a new flavour plus 1% of all future sales. The company www.threadless.com accepts designs for T-shirts, puts them to a public vote and manufactures those with a high approval rating. Most companies are happy to receive suggestions for improvement or new products. If you feel you have a better idea for a TV advert for a particular product then why not email it to the company? What might be the next big successful quiz show format? Why not pitch you winning formula to the BBC? Students might also create resources, mount a display, organise a visit, book a visiting speaker, join school or college management committees, play a part in the Students' Union, organise a competition, enter a regional competition, enter a national competition, contribute to the VLE, make a video, design a Powerpoint, made a podcast etc. Ultimately our aim is to encourage our students to explore their subjects in depth, to consider practical applications and to play a full part in the life of the school or college and their local community. Creativity is about challenge and an opportunity to encourage and stretch the most able in particular.

Targets and assessment

This section of the Portal can identify formal assessment requirements linked to the topic along with appropriate guidance and deadlines.

Many staff issue 'assessment briefs' and marking plans and this should be encouraged so that students are fully aware of the assessment demands. A link to the Individual Learning Plan (ILP) might also be useful and ideally an electronic learning plan for ease of access by all relevant staff.

Pass question and challenge questions.

The difference between pass and challenge is significant because it goes to the heart of effective differentiation. The intention is to make differentiation explicit and 'visible' so that students are aware of the standards applied by examiners to their course programme. Essentially all students should know what the minimum standards are in terms of the knowledge and skills required to secure, at least, a pass and equally what the examination board or assessor expects for the award of a high grade or a distinction. All should be able to answer the pass questions and if uncertain to seek and find the answers they need from the Core Knowledge resources, the wider internet, their mentor, Learning Centre staff, their peers or their teacher etc. Students must be encouraged to take some responsibility for their own learning and to take positive actions to ensure they can at least answer the pass level questions. Equally all students should engage with the challenge questions as far as possible with awareness that they represent a higher standard. They should enter lessons ready to seek confirmation of the answers and to raise and discuss their own uncertainties and hopefully follow and understand the explanations provided. Meta-cognition relates to developing the ability of students' to self-assess, plan, monitor and evaluate their own work and to seek and act on improvement guidance. All our students should be encouraged to reflect on what they know and equally what they don't know. In the case of a vocational pass / fail course the challenge level may be translated to target commercial standards or even world class standards as evidenced by the World Skills championships detailed in Chapter Five.

Setting a strategy

The above features of effective VLE practice are far from unique to the Collegenet Learning Portal. There are very similar 'home-grown' developments in many schools and colleges and a wealth of commercial 'learning platform' software to select from plus a choice of tools embedded in interactive whiteboards. However, what is lacking in many colleges and schools is a clear VLE development strategy linked to classroom practice. When navigating many colleges and school VLEs it quickly becomes apparent that:

- Students do not receive uniform support – some course areas have evidence of significant online resources and others do not,
- Students do not receive uniform communication – some areas use text, email, Q&A forums and others do not,
- Resources are often context free i.e. not linked to Schemes of Work, learning targets, classroom topics and assessment,
- Resources are often presented in a random list of folders with no common layout to aid navigation,
- There is no common pedagogy as to how the resources advance learning or link to classroom practice,
- VLE resources are regarded as additional to classroom practice rather than central to it,
- the VLE development is ad-hoc with any developments largely the product of individual enthusiasts rather than a planned and monitored strategy.

The movement of the curriculum online should be a high priority for all schools and colleges to underpin independent learning and to deliver the skills and knowledge required for living and working in the 21st Century.

9 Coaching independent learning

'For thirty-seven years I've practiced fourteen hours a day, and now they call me a genius'.

Spanish Violinist Pablo de Sarasate (1844-1908)[1]

The i-learning model promotes learners as active participants in their own learning who will engage in online research and interact with others outside of the classroom to drive forward their own learning. Some students are naturally independent learners who regardless of technology have always studied outside of the classroom and dived below the surface information into deeper and wider exploration of their key topics. They tend to possess higher than average motivation and effective study skills and consistently deliver high achievement rates because they cover much more of the curriculum and to a greater depth. Essentially our most successful students invest much more time and effort. However, the reality of our classrooms is that most students struggle to find the motivation and/or lack the skills to advance their own learning. The majority of students (the silent middle) tend to be *dependent learners* i.e. they wait to be given information and seldom undertake independent study outside of the classroom. A minority, the *directed learners* may also exhibit disaffection, play truant and need regular firm direction and additional support to fulfil minimum study expectations. Our significant goal is to draw into active participation the majority *dependent* and *directed* learners to fully embrace independent learning and to develop and apply the learning strategies employed by their more successful peers. The onset of the i-learning revolution offers us significant new tools and greater opportunities for personalised learning support to develop all as effective and successful independent learners. This will require not just the provision of a Learning Portal and a reliable IT infrastructure but a concerted focus to build and coach the skills of independent learning and not just for exam success but to equip for future university and later employment. The factors underpinning successful learning are many and complex but in 2009 Professor John Hattie of Auckland University, New Zealand cut the Gordian Knot. Hattie analysed the outcomes of over 800 peer reviewed research studies into effective teaching and learning and scored each one with an 'effect size'. [2] An effect size of 0.4 or above was identified as an indicator of a strategy with a significant influence on learning and Hattie identified 66 strategies above this threshold and linked them to six key learning influences i.e. home, teacher, teaching, curricula, school and student. Of the six influences the skills of the individual teacher were identified as the most significant factor to drive forward achievement. All of the other factors were secondary and Hattie concluded that the key issue for achievement wasn't which school or college you went to but which classroom you ended up in. The significant skill of an effective teacher was the ability to question and pinpoint individual misunderstandings and to provide sufficient overlapping examples and explanations until the 'penny dropped'. The i-learning pedagogy anticipates learning support from peers, mentors, teaching assistants and Learning Centre staff etc in addition to the teacher and so hopefully there will be multiple opportunities for the penny to drop. Hattie's conclusion was confirmed by the 2007 McKinsey report, 'How the world's best performing school-systems come out on top' [3] which highlighted the need to not only appoint the best qualified applicants but to grow and develop their skills to be effective instructors and finally to, 'raise the standard of every student'.[4] The latter point is key to the i-learning pedagogy. Schools and colleges need to grow the skills of all students to take advantage of flexible online learning opportunities and to become effective independent learners.

Raising the standard of every student

All too often we detect low study skills, low motivation, low self-esteem and sometimes unsupportive home environments but our interventions are often sporadic and ineffective. All staff need to be conscious of the need to act in a consistent way to address individual barriers to learning including the consistent application of behaviour codes with clear and enforced boundaries by all staff. Hattie's survey concluded that students need to 'buy into' the benefits of learning, to maintain full attendance, to invest time to learn and to appreciate that achievement is linked to effort rather than being clever. The related

134

key strategies, identified by Hattie with scores above the 0.40 threshold, were as follows in ascending order:[5]

- actions to reduce *anxiety* 0.40,
- building *self-concept* 0.43 i.e. a personal role identification as a learner and a commitment to investing time in learning,
- promoting *motivation* 0.48,
- encouraging *concentration and persistence* 0.48,
- gaining *parental involvement* 0.51
- issuing and monitoring challenging *goals* scored 0.56.
- supportive *home environment* 0.57
- teaching *study skills* 0.59
- Developing *creativity* 0.65 i.e. activities and structured support to prompt higher order thinking and reasoning skills
- Developing *meta-cognitive strategies* 0.69 i.e. self-assessment, review, self-questioning and seeking and acting on improvement guidance.
- *Teacher-student relationships* 0.72 i.e. empathy, listening, high expectations
- how to improve *feedback* 0.73
- *Teacher clarity* 0.75 i.e. in terms of learning intentions and success criteria

The above strategies all overlap and intertwine and the findings may be best summarised by the following three core strategies as a focus for development actions.

Why learn...?	What to learn...?	How to learn...?
Aim to raise motivation and personal ambition by 'selling' the benefits of your subject.	Offer clear guidance to the major topics, exam format and monitor clear targets.	Instruct and model how to research, write, calculate and present etc.
<ul><li>Employment options</li><li>University options</li><li>Role models</li><li>Current research</li><li>Motivational displays</li><li>Visiting speakers</li><li>Raising self-belief</li></ul>	<ul><li>Specification details</li><li>Advance organisers</li><li>VLE support e.g. Learning Portal</li><li>Exam requirements</li><li>Past exam papers</li><li>Peer sharing</li></ul>	<ul><li>Organisational/study skills</li><li>Time management</li><li>Writing frames/templates</li><li>Exemplars</li><li>Peer support</li><li>Home support</li><li>Applying effort</li></ul>

Why learn...?

The students of the Urban Prep Boys School in Chicago start each day with a recital of their personal creed, *"We are the young men of Urban Prep. We are college bound. We are exceptional – not because we say it but because we work hard at it. We believe in ourselves. We believe in each other. We believe in Urban Prep"* [6]Too many of our students lack ambition and a clear awareness of the different career opportunities, including self-employment, linked to their course of study. Despite the best efforts of our career service many pupils receive insufficient careers guidance and may enter a course of study with very limited horizons and limited ideas of where it might lead. In the internet era with its low start-up costs self employment is a real possibility. Abi Wright was discouraged from entering business by a careers adviser but founded www.spabreaks.com and today employs 35 staff and enjoys a turnover of £7 million per year. Those with parent(s) or guardian(s) who have been to university and/or held regular employment or established their own business tend to hold the advantage because they can offer significant guidance and support to their children. They also tend to place a high value on education and promote and expect progression to university. Therefore from first interview and induction forward it is important to ensure that all students have a sense of purpose, a career goal or at least a significant interest in their chosen course. To combat low or uncertain careers goals we need to promote ambition by raising awareness of the knowledge and skills the students will gain and the range of future career opportunities. Course titles like Biology, Business Studies or Engineering may not convey much to a student in terms of opportunity but if the classroom wall has a list of 50 associated jobs with examples of salaries, major employers, role models, university options, current research etc the subject becomes much more meaningful and our students might develop greater ambition and establish personal goals. Within the Motor Vehicle field the future is electric with the all-electric Nissan Leaf winning the Car of the Year award 2011. Within Biology In-vitro technology is set to produce meat grown from animal cells in the laboratory and eventually replace animals in the field. Within Physics the Cern project is questioning Einstein's theory of Relativity etc. What are the 'big questions' in your subject? Referencing current research often makes a good lesson 'appetiser' or starter activity to make links to the world of work, new developments or university cutting edge research. Invite your students to maintain a current affairs learning wall in your classroom and prompt greater application by organising appropriate visits, invite into classrooms role models and past students, advertise local, regional and national competitions and organise creative and challenge events. The BBC Business News editor Robert Peston has established the website speakers4schools.org to offer schools and colleges leading national figures across most subject areas to inspire young people to be the best they can be. Essentially the most effective schools and colleges aim to inspire and raise personal horizons and ambition because it drives effort and ultimately achievement.

What to learn…?

Independent learners are well organised and tend to examine the specification, the examination requirements, past exam papers, the marking criteria and the relative importance of each key topic and this 'strategic' planning is a major factor in their success. However, the *dependent* and *directed* learners tend to lack the skill and confidence to source this depth of information and to know what to study and in what order and to what depth. Their parents may also not have studied at a higher level and lack the knowledge or ability to offer helpful guidance of how to find information or even the confidence to ask teachers for further information. Course specifications are also not the most illuminating of documents and are often too formal for students to unpick in terms of precise study goals. Equally staff Schemes of Work, even if shared with students, may lack sufficient clarity of what to study. The majority of our students need much more structured support in terms of the key topics and associated resources in order to study ahead and to develop independent learning skills. Without clarity of 'what to learn' students are made dependent on the weekly lesson for their information and support and we may find ourselves building and supporting dependency rather than independence. In the Knowledge Age the Virtual Learning Environment (VLE) is the significant vehicle for sharing and accessing information and the Learning Portal as described in Chapter Eight is one recommended means of providing topic by topic study guidance. The term 'advance organiser' is a descriptive term often applied to guidance on 'what to learn' and some form of advance organiser is a vital support tool to underpin independent study. This clarity of 'what to learn' should also extend into the classroom with the sharing of explicit objectives or better still key questions so that the students are in no doubt as to what they are going to learn and the associated success criteria.

How to learn...?

Coaching how to learn is the third and often most significant teaching function to build the skills of independent learning. Our *directed learners*, in particular, lack effective study skills and may need our help with quite basic aspects like time management and how to maintain a file etc. Model how to maintain a file or how to structure an essay or report or even specify the minimum study kit of A4 paper, pen, pencil, calculator etc. as required. To be effective there should be common staff expectations so that students receive consistent messages in relation to how their work should be presented and completed. Publish standard behavioural contracts and consistently enforce your non-negotiable minimum standards and identify 'at risk' students who may need rapid intervention to cope with the course. The simple provision of standard writing frames or how to lay out an assignment can make the difference for many students. Exemplar answers can also be of significant help to illustrate what a good answer looks like. It is common on many courses for higher marks to be awarded for writing that is analytical and evaluative in style and lower marks for writing that is largely descriptive. However, how is this difference shared with students and how are all coached to improve their writing to the higher standard? Without explicit exemplars and 'how to learn' support and guidance many students will not achieve as well as they might and those on the margins of pass/fail may end up on the wrong side. It is notable that the expansion of Higher Education in the UK has been accompanied by a significant increase in the number of 'drop outs' because too many students lack effective study skills and the skills to be independent learners. This is a significant teaching function but one that is often neglected and/or relegated to the tutorial session. All staff should teach relevant 'how to learn' skills in context as they approach each significant task or topic. This includes how to present which is a vital skill for the workplace and wider life. Too many teachers watch clearly nervous young people struggling to give a presentation but fail to coach body language, voice projection, breathing techniques, use of cue cards, visual slides etc. to help them develop the skills of confident public speaking. Confidence is not something we are born with but it is something we can develop with help. However, the key intervention is to ensure that all students are applying sufficient effort to succeed and to comment upon and measure effort at relevant assessment points.

Overall strategies

The overall strategies to lift the performance of each broad group of learners may be summarised as follows:

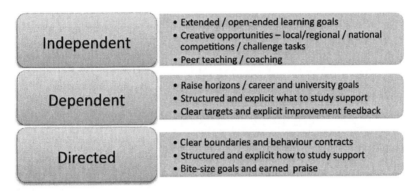

The above strategies are not exhaustive or exclusive to each group but they are the core strategies to advance the learning and skills of each group. Differentiation is a continuum and we ideally present open-ended learning opportunities and coach students to apply the maximum effort. Each student is an individual and we need to quickly move beyond the above broad labels to build the ambition, learning skills, and employability skills of each individual and help them to overcome their personal barriers to learning as they move through the curriculum. Hence the central importance of the targets set within an Individual Learning Plan (ILP) and the attachment of a Learning Mentor to steer and guide progress and of most importance timely interventions by mentors to build self-belief and to convert 'can't do' into 'can do with help'. Overall an individual who feels a sense of purpose and progress will attend, participate and ultimately achieve. This links to the issue of Hattie's highest scoring strategy of all 'self-report grades' which scored 1.44 well above the 0.40 threshold. [7] The research findings are closely allied to research into *self-concept*

and taken together describe how students ascribe to themselves an ability ranking against their peers and adopt an opinion of their personal standing within each subject. This personal ranking, whether high or low, is linked to either increasing or decreasing motivation. Essentially students know when they are finding something difficult. They do not need to wait to receive a grade from their teacher hence *self- report grades.* It is common to overhear students remarking this is a hard subject but that subject is easy or this topic is very difficult or, 'I don't get algebra' etc. In the introductory classroom scenes of the Channel Four TV programme 'Educating Essex' broadcast in Autumn 2011, a student in a Maths lesson says with frustration, *'What is pie? I don't get pie? Where did pie come from?'* However, her remarks were not made to the teacher but to a friend who offered no enlightenment because she too was obviously uncertain. The reluctance of most students to seek help underlines the significance of employing 'assessment for learning' techniques during lessons to gain feedback, to uncover misunderstandings and to offer regular opportunities for difficulties to be expressed. What have the students found 'hard' and what 'don't they get'? Unpacking and correcting individual misunderstandings via brief one to one chats and careful question and answer are all key to countering self-report grades. This underpins the recommended strategy of using the Learning Portal (Chapter Eight) to absorb core factual information outside of the lesson thereby reserving the lesson time for individual, paired and group tasks to facilitate a regular learning dialogue. Gaining feedback from students about what they are finding difficult is part of this learning dialogue and scores 0.73 in Hattie's hierarchy and this raises the associated skill of building an effective supportive student-teacher relationship i.e. the ability to display empathy, to listen, to avoid sarcasm and above all to offer clear stepping stones to help each student to move forward. Students who identify their performance as low in relation to their peers often accept their personal ranking as fixed and do not actively seek ways to improve. Teachers also rank performance and like students may 'assign' rankings and anticipate the mark before reading the assignment. The counter is to de-personalise marking by marking against standard marking criteria to ensure feedback that details how marks were won or lost. It also builds confidence because it is common for students to discover that different staff mark and correct different things and that marks appear to be idiosyncratic rather to a

book any holidays in term time and support the completion of homeworks. The contracts clearly work. In summer 2011 82% of the pupils gained five GCSE grades A*-C including Maths and English and 91% without. This is one of the highest performance records of any school in England and even more impressive given the high levels of deprivation within the local area. A total of 40% of the pupils are eligible for Free School Meals (FSM) which is a significant indicator of low income and potential learning disadvantage. The headteacher Sir Michael Wilshaw was knighted in 2000 for his services to education and teachers might welcome his appointment in 2011 as the Chief Inspector of Ofsted given his exemplary record of putting policy into action. The headteacher of Burlington Danes Academy in West London, Sally Coates has a similar reputation for enforcing high standards and overriding disadvantage with a 'can do' expectation. The numbers of pupils attending the school eligible for Free School Meals is three times the national average and in summer 2011 75% gained five GCSES grades A*-C including English and Maths also significantly above the national average of 56.1% (without inclusion of iGCSE). The most fundamental and obvious first step in terms of successful engagement is to hold high expectations and to identify the school or college as a portal to a better future. Education and qualifications offer all a common pathway to personal satisfaction and greater prosperity regardless of background. Consequently high expectations must be translated into action in terms of attendance, effort and aspirations. Celebrate and expect 100% attendance not 85% or even 99%. Low attendance is often a symptom of not valuing school and this in turn often reveals pupils or students who are not making progress. This returns us to the concept of *self-report grades* because our students know if they are making progress or not and when they decide they are not they tend to truant rather than address their learning difficulties. It is highly important that all pupils and students gain a sense of progress. Therefore formative assessment systems should include an early warning of underperformance with rapid interventions by mentors when performance slips. Finally, our students should be tasked with applying sufficient effort to succeed with regular checks that independent learning tasks have been completed and that the online Learning Portal resources have been viewed and the checklists of linked key questions answered. Associated with this is a firm zero tolerance behaviour policy which is consistently enforced by all rather than by some staff. Overall our goal is to ensure that students leave each lesson and end each day with a sense of progress because this will feed greater effort. Once students gain the self-belief that their knowledge and skills are growing lesson by lesson they will not only attend but apply themselves further. Additionally once they know that any breaches of the behaviour contract will result in sanctions the significant majority will conform. Our overall aim should be to develop a sustained learning dialogue that not only motivates and coaches improvement but gives each student a real sense of personal progress. The significance of these factors to promoting effective teaching and learning was confirmed in May 2011 by the research organisation the Sutton Trust (suttontrust.org). The Sutton Trust published a 'toolkit' review of the most effective teaching and learning strategies in 2011 and largely confirmed the earlier research findings published by Hattie. The Sutton Trust's top three strategies for *'very high impact at low cost'* improvements to teaching and learning were:

- Effective feedback
- Meta-cognition
- Peer tutoring / peer assisted learning

The findings all tend to endorse constructivist strategies as the core of successful learning i.e. building students' awareness of their own progress, identifying barriers to learning and providing support. The core process of learning is one of repetition and consolidation of key information via regular recap, question and answer, individual tasks, paired tasks and group tasks. New learning is essentially absorbed by forming personal constructs and moving from what is known to what is unknown. Effective teachers focus more on learning outcome rather than information input and the significant action is to help students to understand and apply concepts and to move, in constructivist terms, from concrete to abstract reasoning.

Applying constructivism

Constructivism arises from the work of Jean Piaget (1896-1980). Piaget was a Swiss biologist who studied child development and defined the following four stages of cognitive development.

Stage	Age	Characteristics
Sensorimotor	0-2	Children actively explore their world by touching, smelling, tasting, listening and most of all by watching. They watch and copy.
Pre-operational	3-7	Regular egocentric behaviour focussed on wants, testing of boundaries, asking why and gradual recognition and acceptance of limits.
Concrete operational	8-11	Rationalisation of their environment and development of a base of factual, concrete knowledge and reasoning.
Formal operational	12+	Questioning their environment and adding new knowledge / observations and applying theoretical and abstract reasoning and arriving at personal constructs.

Piaget's four stages provide a compelling framework for how our ability to think and learn develops as we interact with the world around us. In terms of advancement the key hurdle is the transition between the last two stages and the movement from concrete to abstract reasoning. Many young people struggle to apply propositions or to conceptualise explanations which may conflict with their own experience and their established opinion of what is correct or notions of right and wrong. Interestingly the influence of peers overtakes family at the fourth stage and there is much truth in the parental warning of falling into 'bad company'. This tends to explain the emergence of different development pathways by children from the same home despite exposure to the same values and environment. It is common for students to express frustration when presented with information or opinions which conflict with their own beliefs or accepted knowledge. They may not want to engage with the issue and think about and analyse the concept because it confers a sense of instant confusion and many may request just to be told the 'right answer'. Coaching students to move from factual, concrete surface reasoning i.e. less *what* and more *why* is a difficult challenge but a significant one because high exam marks are reserved for higher order thinking and reasoning. Hattie ranks *Piagetian programmes* as second in the overall hierarchy of effective teaching and learning strategies with a score of 1.28. To gain higher level marks students must develop the ability to analyse and evaluate rather than to just describe and explain. We can assist this process by expanding upon lesson aims and objectives with a 'big picture' introduction so that students appreciate the relationship between different aspects of their studies and gain clear objectives and success criteria to guide their learning. This explicit guidance is referred to as *teacher clarity* and scores 0.75 in Hattie's hierarchy of effective learning strategies. Hattie also highlights that many students benefit from visual representation and therefore the 'big picture' overview might be reinforced by using mind mapping diagrams, spider diagrams or Smartart diagrams to display objectives or preferably key questions. The use of visuals in general to support learning or *concept mapping* scored 0.57 in Hatties' hierarchy. Once the big picture has been absorbed lessons should focus on individual, paired and group tasks to give time to explore the new learning in more depth and sufficient opportunities for reflection and individual and small group coaching support. The significant aim is to open a learning dialogue with students in terms of what they understand and of greater importance what they do not understand and to reinforce the concept of effort over ability.

Engaging adults

Adults are often perceived as being wholly different to younger students in their approaches to learning hence we talk of andragogy (man leading) rather than pedagogy (child leading) but there are perhaps more commonalities than differences. The essential difference is that adults have acquired a wider and deeper set of experiences which have shaped their opinions and views and as a consequence they may often hold entrenched opinions of their abilities. Hence we return to statements like *I can't do…? or I'm no good at ..?* The act of enrolment in adult education tends to confirm this proposition in terms of a personally identified learning deficit i.e. a qualification or learning not gained at school. In this context there may be a negative mindset of *'can't do'* which is an immediate barrier to learning rather than the acknowledgement of missed learning opportunities or unfavourable learning circumstances. However, many adults are also very successful learners who are returning to the classroom to gain new skills to enhance their leisure, employment or life. Life experience in either case can manifest itself in fairly fixed opinions and attitudes that have been consolidated and unchallenged over time by family and peer group and this may lead to discomfort with alternative propositions. In addition, many adults may feel vulnerable in returning to lessons because the action cedes control to a teacher and rather than choosing to do something they may be asked to answer a question or to move into pairs or to write something or to complete a calculation. Directed tasks of this type can raise 'completion anxiety' essentially the fear of giving a wrong answer and so often adult students seek not participative learning but more formalised or directive learning i.e. rather than risk an answer or an opinion they wish the teacher to state the 'correct' answer to record. This preference for direction is most often a reflection of past school experience when perhaps lessons were fairly didactic with a process of 'chalk and talk' or direct copying of notes from a board. To assist adult learners to see the value of participative learning the following three strategies are useful:

- Explain the **purpose** of the activity e.g. why do you wish them to work in pairs? What they will gain from this activity and how it will help to improve their understanding and learning? Adults will accept an active learning task when they appreciate the point and purpose i.e. it is not just a game or activity for the sake of it but there is a serious underpinning purpose in terms of what they will discover, learn and gain.
- Establish **relevance** of the tasks or learning approaches or assessment activities in relation to the exam requirements, skill requirements or wider work requirements or employability skills development. Once adults 'buy-in' to how the task fulfils exam or employability requirements they are again more likely to participate.
- Ensure **choice** over aspects of the curriculum, timings and sequence of topics and learning activities but choice that still builds in a variety of active learning approaches i.e. the choice is between a discussion in pairs or movement into a group or studying X before break or after break. Offering all students, but

adults in particular, some semblance of control will assist all to feel more relaxed and encourage participation.

Applying *purpose, relevance* and *choice* will assist the learning process but like younger students be alert to individual progress. Adults will not return and commit themselves to learning if they judge that a new skill is too difficult and so ensure that the first sessions introduce bite-size learning and immediate, positive 'can do' experiences.

Vygotsky's Zone of Proximal Development (ZPD)

A key extension of this thinking was provided by Lev Vygotsky (1896-1934) arising from his work as a psychologist in the Moscow Institute of Psychology during the late 1920s. Vygotsky postulated the theory of the Zone of Proximal Development (ZPD) which essentially addressed the fundamental difference between *'can do'* and *'can't do'*. In other words self-belief. Vygotsky articulated that the inner voice of *'can't do'* was a significant barrier to learning especially when students expressed opinions like, *'I'm no good at maths, I can't do maths'*. Vygotsky addressed this fundamental issue of self-belief by offering the positive proposition of *'can do'* and *'can do with help'*. It is a simple construct but one that if applied can empower students to accept that their ability is not fixed but moveable with help. This reasoning was significantly extended by the work of Professor Carol Dweck of Stanford University in 1987 with controlled experiments in relation to effort and intelligence. Dweck identified the tendency of many students to ascribe their low progress in a given subject to an innate inability to understand maths or science or English etc. rather than a measure of time and effort applied. Dweck defined two predominant attitudes in relation to achievement, *Fixed IQ* and *Untapped potential*. Those who fall into the 'Fixed IQ' mindset believe that it is all in the genes i.e. a fixed ability whereas those with an 'Untapped potential' or a 'growth mindset' are open to the idea of seeking support and applying effort to succeed. Dweck recommended that teachers praise effort and the time invested rather than ability or intelligence i.e. not so much 'oh you are really clever' but rather, 'you must have worked really hard on this'. Dweck's guidance was confirmed by the most recent PISA international study of student achievement. In 2011 PISA tracked the most successful students from disadvantaged backgrounds in relation to successful progress in science lessons and observed that the common characteristic was 'resilience'. The successful students maintained higher rates of attendance and *'the more self-confident students are, the greater their odds of being resilient....Some 75% of resilient students believed they can give good answers to test questions...'* [8] The readiness of many students to say 'can't do' is closely linked to popular concepts of intelligence and the belief that you are either born clever or you are not.

Where are we with intelligence?

The nature or nurture debate has dominated educational debate ever since the British psychologist Charles Spearman in 1904 reported a correlation between individual students and their consistently high or low performance across unrelated subjects. Spearman concluded that each student's consistent either high or low performance was evidence of general intelligence or the G Factor. Around the same time, in France, Alfred Binet devised the first IQ test to identify pupils who would benefit from extra learning assistance. Binet's concept of a helpful diagnostic tool was elevated into a formal categorisation of intelligence by the Director of Psychology at Stanford University Lewis Terman (1877-1956). In 1916 Terman published the Stanford-Binet IQ test which today, after several revisions, remains the dominant test of IQ. Terman established an IQ of 100 as a norm and 140+ as an indicator of genius whereas IQs below 80 descended into degrees of cognitive deficiency. In 1921 Terman set out to demonstrate that genes governed intelligence by embarking upon a longitudinal study of 1528 people with an IQ of 140+ i.e. genius level. Terman's *'Genetic studies of Genius'* project tracked the lives and careers of all 1528 subjects but to his disappointment, although the majority established comfortable academic careers, none became acknowledged leaders in their fields. In fact two children, William Shockley and Luis Alvarez who Terman had originally tested but rejected for admittance to his genius group, because their IQ levels were below the 140 threshold, went on to separately win Nobel Prizes for Physics. During the peak career window of Terman's genius group the notable advances in sciences, humanities, engineering, politics etc. arose from individuals, with IQs lower than 140, outside of the genius group. Some of the genius group also entered low level occupations and overall the progress of the genius group reflected what might be expected from any cross section of middle class society.

The outcome of the genius study reinforces the view that there is a threshold for intelligence and beyond this threshold other factors related to nurture and opportunity drive success. The reliability of IQ tests and how far intelligence is a product of inheritance or environment remains a divisive topic. The two polar extremes of the debate were in evidence in January 2011. First Amy Chua an American mother of Chinese heritage published an account of how she raised her two daughters entitled, 'The *battle hymn of the tiger mother'.*[9] Secondly, Bryan Caplan an American economics professor at George Mason University published, *'Selfish reasons to have more kids'.* [10] Chua emphasised effort and detailed her relentless regime of dawn to dusk pressure on her children to study with an insistence that Grade B was never good enough. The polar opposite opinion was presented by Caplan who drew upon studies of the cognitive performance of identical twins who were separated at birth and adopted by different families. The twins, reunited as adults, consistently scored in intelligence tests at the same level as their birth mothers rather than their adoptive parents and despite spending their formative years in different home environments. Caplan concluded that intelligence is 'written' i.e. it is all in the genes and that our actions as parents will have no impact on achievement. Clearly there must be a middle ground between the two extremes. The most recent research published by the University of Edinburgh in August 2011 identified over 600,000 aspects of gene activity that contribute to cognitive ability. The study by Professor Ian Dreary concluded that genes account for 50% of our cognitive ability and nurture 50%. The evidence points to a common cognitive threshold or capacity to learn which subsequent environment influences can either expand or degrade. The conclusion that IQ may not be fixed is also strengthened by the so called Flynn effect named after Professor James Flynn of Otago University, New Zealand. Flynn charted evidence of a steady rise in IQ levels over the last century. The evidence came to light because IQ tests are norm referenced and Flynn observed that the companies involved were resetting the norm level for each generation to give consistent variables. In theory each generation was becoming more intelligent and this gave rise to two propositions: either selective breeding of the human population or improvements in learning. The generational difference is around 15 points and it is speculated that the greater exposure of children to television, radio, advertising, books, games, computers, quizzes and perhaps greater familiarity sentiment and it highlights that care must be taken in our schools and colleges to qualify the achievements of 'gifted and talented' students because of a common assumption of a genetic predisposition rather than hard work. Ericsson's message as detailed in his 2006 publication, *The Cambridge Handbook of Expertise and Expert Performance*[12] is that we can all become gifted and talented with sufficient effort. Genius is not always what it seems. Wolfgang Amadeus Mozart was and is celebrated as a genius because he played the piano at the age of 6 and composed his first piano concerto at the age of 11. However, what is often unreported is that Mozart's father was Leopold Mozart an accomplished composer, musician and performer feted across Europe. The young Mozart was coached to play the piano, from the age of 3, by his father who was one of the foremost musicians in Europe and on a daily basis rather than for just a few hours per week. By the time Mozart released his first original composition Piano Concerto No. 9 at the comparatively young age of 21 he had put in 18 years of continuous daily practice and effort to perfect his music. Mozart's success was not an innate talent but coached perfection. Genius evaporates when you ask any top ranked scientist, sports star, writer, inventor, business leader etc how many hours they put in. Thomas A Edison (1847-1931) famously remarked, *'genius is one percent inspiration and ninety-nine percent perspiration.'* [13] Ericsson calculated that to be exceptional i.e. to achieve first ranking in world class standards required 10,000 hours of effort. To be considered highly proficient or 'good' on a world class basis 8,000 hours and to be able to teach and coach others at least 6,000 hours of continuous effort to refine and perfect the relevant skills and knowledge.

Independent learning

All of this returns us to the importance of independent learning to boost achievement and the moot question is how many hours of study do your students put in and how many should they put in? Ideally our students should treat their full-time courses as their full-time jobs and put in a 40 hour week minimum. In general terms for every hour in the classroom there should be a minimum of one hour of study outside the classroom. However, what should they do outside the classroom? The i-learning pedagogy of transferring resources to a Learning Portal with clear guidance on what to study will provide the structure that so many students need and with firm as students gain learning support from Learning Centre staff, teaching assistants, mentors, parents, neighbours, youth workers, etc and the ever expanding internet. Few will undertake research to the extent of Augusto Odone but students will gain much more autonomy in terms of what and when to learn and step out of often unruly classrooms where teachers struggle to keep order into individual learning programmes. Teachers will define themselves less as the gatekeepers of a particular set of facts and knowledge and more in terms of their ability to explain, illustrate and assist young people to understand and to extend their learning. Virtual Learning Environments (VLE) like the Learning Portal will capture and hold recommended resources topic by topic and allow teachers to draw from the best of the internet and reliable academic sources. Every year thousands of Business Studies teachers design and prepare lessons on Sole Traders and many thousands of History teachers design and prepare lessons on Bismarck's foreign policy etc. All are operating in parallel perhaps within the same school, or in neighbouring schools, or across their region or the whole country in a significant duplication of effort. Some of those lessons and related resources are first class but others are not and our students take their chances lesson by lesson. The capture of first class resources will end the lottery of the well prepared as against the poorly prepared lesson and offer all teachers and students a common platform of high quality learning resources. In this regard the highly popular khanacademy.org offers a significant collection of videos (as described in Chapter Six) and a potent illustration of a horizontal development. The Khan Academy was not developed by a teacher or a teacher trainer, or a professor of education or a consultant, or a writer of textbooks but by Salman Khan a Hedge Fund Analyst of Mountain View, California. In 2004 Salman responded to his cousin Nadia's request for help with her maths homework by recording short videos to coach her on key topics. The videos proved so popular with her friends that they ended up on You Tube and from that base there are now 2,600 videos covering a wide range of subjects and growing. This is our i-learning future as creative people whether teachers or not develop and share first class resources. Teachers are by instinct very creative and with opportunities to be creative they can soon produce their own videos and other resources and source the best of the web and share for the benefit of all. VLEs have an unlimited capacity to hold and deliver structured learning programmes and will never tire of repeating the same information and thereby reduce lesson preparation time and release teachers to focus on coaching learning. In 1850 the Government in response to the first revolution in communication passed the Public Libraries Act to ensure all citizens had access to books. Perhaps it is time for the Public Broadband Act or for an even greater leap forward the Public 4G Act to facilitate the i-learning revolution.

Appendix

 Digital skills questionnaire

The digital skills questionnaire may be adopted or adapted, as thought appropriate, and should be used to raise a discussion with students about their levels of ICT skills and to inform ICT support and development opportunities within course programmes. It should be a clear goal for all schools and colleges to embed and build a wide range of digital competencies.

Digital skills survey

With the fast expansion of online resources for learning and the demand by employers and universities for high levels of 'digital skills' it is important that while at college you develop and improve your digital skills. To help us plan opportunities to help you build and extend your digital skills please complete this survey.

Main course_____

Age group 14-15 / 16-18 / 19-24 / 25+

Please tick either yes or no to the following questions

1. Computer equipment	Yes	No
Do you have a desk top / tower computer at home?		
Do you have a laptop computer at home?		
Do you have a tablet computer at home e.g. ipad?		
Do you have a mobile phone?		
Do you have a dedicated e-book reader e.g. Kindle?		

2. Internet connection(s)	Yes	No
Do you have a home broadband connection?		
Do you have a laptop with an internet connection either wifi or permanent e.g. 3G connection?		
Do you have a Smart mobile phone i.e. internet linked?		
Do you have an internet linked television?		

3. Internet usage	Yes	No
Do you have a personal email address?		
Do you have a Facebook account or similar social network?		
Do you have a Twitter account?		
Do you have a blog?		
Do you have your own website?		
Do you have a cloud account for storing files/ data?		
Do you have RSS update feeds from favourite websites?		

Please enter a score from 1 low to 5 high for each question

4. Online activity	Score
How would you rate your general use of the internet? What is your score for using the internet for each of the following activities:	
Emailing	
Instant messaging	
Visiting social networking site e.g Facebook	
Downloading music	
Downloading books	
Downloading films	
Downloading software	
Playing games	
Researching coursework or homework	
Preparing / completing coursework or homework	
Visiting news websites e.g. BBC, Sky	
Visiting sports websites	
Visiting You Tube	
Buying goods from online traders or shops e.g. Amazon	
Buy apps from itunes or marketplace	
phone texting	
Using Skype or similar video calling / chatting facility	
Watching TV online e.g. iplayer or similar	
Using the college learning portal to find / check information	

Please enter a score from 1 low to 5 high in terms of your general familiarity and ability to use each program.

5. Using Microsoft Office programs	Score
Word	
Powerpoint	
Excel	
Publisher	
Access	
Outlook	

6. Basic level ICT tasks	Yes	Yes With help
Search the internet for information		
Download files or programs from the internet		
Attach a file to an email message		
Download music from the internet		
Write and send an email		
Chat online		
Use a wordprocessor e.g. to write an essay / report		

7. High level ICT tasks	Yes	Yes With help
Use software to find or get rid of viruses		
Create a database i.e. using Microsoft Access		
Edit digital photographs or other graphic images		
Use a spreadsheet to plot a graph		
Create a presentation i.e. using Microsoft Powerpoint		
Creating a multimedia presentation i.e with sound, pictures and video.		
Construct a web page		
Using an interactive whiteboard e.g. Smartboard		

References

Chapter One
1. www.alvintoffler.net
2. World statistics by GDP, composition by sector, www.cia.gov./library/publications/the-world-factbook , 2010.
3. Abid
4. Department for Business, Innovation and Skills, UK Commission for Employment skills, Skills for Jobs: Today and Tomorrow, www.bis.gov.uk
5. World statistics by GDP, composition by sector, www.cia.gov./library/publications/the-world-factbook ,2010.
6. As above
7. As above
8. QS Quacquarelli Symonds (www.topuniversities.com). Copyright © 2004-2008 QS Quacquarelli Symonds Ltd.
9. www.obamaspeeches.com 21st century schools for 21st century economy 13th march 2006, Chicago.

Chapter Two
1. Ken Olsen President of Digital Equipment 1977www.rinkworks.com/said/predictions.shtml.
2. The connected kingdom, how the internet is transforming the UK economy, 2010, Boston Consulting Group.com

Chapter Three
1. Diehard 4.0, 20th Century Fox, 2007, a description of the character John McClane acted by Bruce Willis
2. Forbes.com, 2011 internet billionaires
3. OECD.org, internet usage survey report
4. Abid
5. Abid
6. Abid
7. BBC News UK School Report survey 24th March 2011 www.bbbc.co.uk/schoolreport

8. Office for national statistics, www.statistics.gov.uk, Mr and Mrs average, May 2011.

9. A vision of students today, www. youtube.com, 2008

10. Ofcom annual report, www.ofcom.org.uk, 2010

11. Silver poll, www.onepoll.com, march 2011

12. Cranfield school of management may 2010 survey 267 children

13. Kids online activities, Mediamark.net, 2007

14. Child of our times, www.bbc.co.uk, 2010

15. www.opinionmatters.co.uk, April 2011

16. press release,www.pixmania.com, 15th November 2008

Chapter Four

1. Henry Royce, www.rolls-roycemotorcars.com/goodwood

2. Skills for Jobs: Today and tomorrow, 2010, www.ukces.org.uk, Pg 7-8

3. Ambition 2020, www.ukces.org.uk, 2010.

4. Ready to grow: education and skills, www.cbi.org, 2010, Pg. 18

5. Review of Vocation education, Wolf Report, March 2011, Pg. 26

6. One North East, www.onenortheast.co.uk, 2010

7. Cities Outlook 2011, www.centreforcities.org, January 2011.

8. Review of Vocational Education, Professor Alison Wolf, March 2011, Pg. 83

9. The importance of teaching, White Paper, Recommendation No. 9, November 2010, Pg. 15.

10. Andreas Schleicher, OECD Education Directorate, www.oecd.org

11. International Baccalaureate website, www.ibo.org.

12. PISA 2009, www.oecd.org

13. Partnership 21 website, www.p21.org

14. Working group on 14-19 reform, Tomlinson, 2004, Recommendation 6 para 63, page 30.

15. Working group on 14-19 reform, Tomlinson, 2004,Tomlinson, Para 73, page 33

16. Cambridge Pre-U, Cambridge international examinations, www.cie.org.uk

17. As above

18. Review of Vocation education, Wolf Report, March 2011.

19. The importance of teaching, White Paper, November 2010,Pg. 44, para 4.21

Chapter Five

1. Hard Times, Charles Dickens, 1853, Oxford Classics,2008, Pg. 7
2. CBI Employers survey, 2011, Exhibit 42 Pg. 38
3. Board of Education, Elementary school code for England, Pg 8.
4. OECD 21st Century skills and competences report
5. OECD IT Skills report
6. Abid pg. 16
7. Abid pg. 30
8. Abid page 32.
9. DFES, Vision 2020, December 2006, www.education.gov.uk
10. Abid, Pg.10
11. Abid, pg.13.
12. www.atcs.org website mission statement
13. KSAVE framework from Skills White Paper www.acts.org
14. CBI, Ready to grow: education and skills, 2010, Pg. 24
15. CBI Building for Growth: education and skills survey ,2011
16. Ofsted inspectors handbook, www.ofsted.gov.uk
17. Department for Education, The importance of teaching: the schools white paper 2010, Pg. 49, Para 4.50
18. World skills, Skills wheel, www.worldskillslondon.com

Chapter Six

1. Obama Senator Barack, Chicago speech, www.obamaspeeches.com, 2006
2. Board of Education, Handbook of suggestions for teachers, 1927, Pg. 13
3. OECD, Are the new millennium learners making the grade, 2010, Pg. 52

Chapter Seven

1. Board of Education, Handbook of suggestions for teachers, 1927, Pg. 24

Chapter Eight

1. old English proverb, author unknown.

Chapter Nine

1. Pablo de Sarasate (1844-1908), The complete pocket positives, Five Mile Press, 2010

2. Hattie, Professor John, Visible Learning: A synthesis of over 800 meta-analyses relating to achievement, Routledge, 2009

3. How the world's best performing school-systems come out on top', McKinsey September 2007

4. Abid. Pg 15

5. Hattie, Professor John, Visible Learning: A synthesis of over 800 meta-analyses relating to achievement, Routledge, 2009, Appendix B

6. Urban Prep Boys' school, school motto, www.urbanprep.org, 2011

7. Hattie, Professor John, Visible Learning: A synthesis of over 800 meta-analyses relating to achievement, Routledge, 2009

8. Pisa, progress in science, www.oecd.org, 2010

9. Chua Amy, the Battle hymn of the tiger mother, 2011

10. Caplan Brian, selfish reasons to have more kids, 2011

11. Pablo de Sarasate (1844-1908), The complete pocket positives, Five Mile Press, 2010

12. Ericsson Anders K (Editor), The Cambridge handbook of expertise and expert performance, Cambridge press, 2006.

13. Edison Thomas, www.brainyquotes.com, 2011

Chapter Ten

1. Laing R.D. www. brainyquotes.com, 2011

In-House Training
504c Huddersfield Road, Ravensthorpe
Dewsbury WF13 3HL
01924 500647
www.in-house-tk13.co.uk
Vat Number 987 981 175   Comp Reg 07512521